D1094436

WITHDRAWN

MAR 0 2 2023

DAVID O. McKAY LIBRARY
BYU-IDAHO

Wood Carving and Whittling Made Easy

FRANKLIN H. GOTTSHALL

ALL DRAWINGS BY THE AUTHOR, FRANKLIN H. GOTTSHALL
PHOTOGRAPHS BY THE AUTHOR AND BY HIS SON, BRUCE H. GOTTSHALL

Macmillan Publishing Co., Inc.
NEW YORK

Collier Macmillan Publishers
LONDON

TO MY WIFE, AGNES

Copyright © 1963 by Franklin H. Gottshall

All rights reserved. No part of this book may be reproduced or transmitted in any form or by any means, electronic or mechanical, including photocopying, recording or by any information storage and retrieval system, without permission in writing from the Publisher.

Library of Congress Catalog Card Number: 63–10891

Macmillan Publishing Co., Inc.
866 Third Avenue
New York, N.Y. 10022
COLLIER-MACMILLAN CANADA LTD.

Sixth Printing 1975

Printed in the United States of America

Contents

Foreword 5

CHAPTER 1

Tools and Equipment for Wood Carving . 7

CHAPTER 2

Methods and Techniques 22

CHAPTER 3

How to Draw Designs and Patterns . . 31

PROJECTS

Bear 33

Stepping Horse 36

Long-Eared Hound 40

Alerted Fawn 43

Feeding Fawn 45

Indian-Head Mask 47

Madonna Shrine 49

Man From the Mennonite Country . . 52

Woman From the Mennonite Country . . 56

Question Mark 60

Bird 62

Spoon Rack and Mirror With Drawer . . 64

3

Table Mats 68

Autumn Harvest 72

Eagle 75

Pop-Up Playing Card Holder . . . 77

Fireplace Bellows 80

The Expanding Bookstall 84

Gothic Box 88

Hand Carved Serving Tray 91

Picture Frames 95

Snack Tray 98

Spice Cabinets 101

Fan-Shaped Box 103

Pipe Holder 105

Bookends With Acanthus Leaf . . . 106

Paper, Letter, and Pencil Holder . . . 109

Carved Box With Beading on Top . . 112

Paper Knife 114

Salad Fork and Salad Spoon . . . 115

Carved Boxes 116

Fruit Bowl 122

Occasional Table 124

Venetian Mirror 127

Foreword

Wood carving can be a most enjoyable hobby; in fact, of the many hobbies which the author has engaged in, wood carving has stood out far and away above all the rest for the satisfactions and sense of achievement it has brought. He heartily recommends it to any home lover for the many satisfying experiences it can bring him. Its decorative value is superb, and possibly even unsurpassed by any other form of craftsmanship. It may be adapted to the decoration of furniture, walls, woodwork, lamps, bric-a-brac, sculpture, and a myriad of other household uses.

For a time, not so long ago, with the advent of modern design, there was some danger of its becoming a lost art, but recently there has been a great revival of interest in this hobby. To this the author can testify personally, judging from the continued popularity of two earlier volumes on wood carving which he has written, or helped to write.

Many people hesitate to take up wood carving as a hobby because they fear it may be too difficult. But actually, what makes this hobby stand out above nearly all other creative hobbies is the ease with which it can be undertaken. One needs but a sharp knife and a small piece of wood to start. Then even the beginner has before him a great variety and diversity of projects. Surprising, too, is the ease and facility with which the neophyte progresses from the very simple to the seemingly more difficult types of carving.

The scope of this wood-carving book includes both relief carving and carving in the round or whittling. In it the author has been mindful of the beginner who needs help in making a start at this most interesting of all creative hobbies. Nor has he neglected the craftsman who has progressed somewhat beyond the beginner's stage. Ultimate usefulness of the objects described has been kept definitely in mind, and there has been a striving for variety and artistic merit.

It is with the sincere hope that these objectives have been achieved, that the author now submits WOOD CARVING AND WHITTLING MADE EASY to his many fellow craftsmen and friends.

FRANKLIN H. GOTTSHALL
Boyertown, Pa.

Acknowledgments

The author is grateful to the following magazines for permission to use projects originally published by them: To *Homecraftsman* for the fireplace bellows, the fruit bowl, and the pop-up playing card holder; to *Industrial Arts and Vocational Education* for the hand carved serving tray.

CHAPTER 1 Tools and Equipment for Wood Carving

The tools needed to do wood carving may consist of only a good pocketknife and the means of sharpening it. Many types of carving may be undertaken, and completely finished right down to the final details by using no other tool except a sharp pocketknife. Whittling is a form of wood carving in which the knife is used exclusively. There is, of course, a haphazard type of whittling, engaged in by some, which results in little more than a pile of shavings. Others have elevated the pastime to the plane of a fine art, and regularly turn out attractive bits of sculpture with a pocketknife. A good pocketknife with a well-sharpened blade or two, is a tool ideally suited to this type of carving, because it may be readily manipulated to make a large variety of cuts. Unlike carving chisels, which are not easily used with one hand alone, the knife may be held with one hand, while the work is turned from one position to another to make cutting easy.

The knife is also a good tool with which to do chip carving.

In Figure 1 are shown four different types of blades, each one very useful to the wood-carver. For heavy, rough cutting such as is done when a carving is started, the spear point, or the clip blade, may be used with good results. The clip blade, provided it is properly sharpened, becomes a good, all-purpose carving blade since its shape is equally well adapted to rough preliminary cutting, known as "boasting-in," or to the finer, more delicate cutting needed to put on the finishing touches.

The pen blade is excellent for getting fine details such as eyes, hairlines, and other delicate cutting. A skew-edged sloyd knife with the blade fixed solidly to the handle will prove to be a very useful tool, not only to the whittler, but to the wood-carver who does most of his carving with chisels. It also is a good tool for chip carving.

While a good pocketknife with one or more sharp blades will prove to be a versatile carving tool, professional wood-carvers, and most amateurs who pursue the craft with some degree of seriousness, soon learn that a set of carving chisels adds immeasurably to

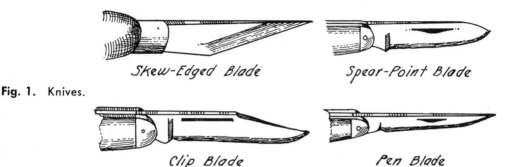

Skew-Edged Blade   *Spear-Point Blade*

Fig. 1. Knives.

Clip Blade   *Pen Blade*

SWEEPS $\frac{1}{16}''$ TO $1\frac{1}{2}''$	NO.	NAME	LONG BENT	SPOON	BACK BENT	V-TOOLS
—	1	CHISELS		21		39 – WIDE
/	2	SKEW		22–23		40 – MEDIUM
—	3	EXTRA-FLAT	12	24	33	41 – NARROW
⌣	4	EXTRA-FLAT	13	25	34	
⌣	5	GOUGES	14	26	35	
⌣	6	GOUGES	15	27	36	
⌣	7	GOUGES	16	28	37	
⌣	8	GOUGES	17	29	38	
⌣	9	GOUGES	18	30		
⌣	10	DEEP GOUGE	19	31		
⌣	11	DEEP GOUGE	20	32		
U	11	FLUTER				
V	11	VEINER				

Fig. 2. Table of chisels and gouges.

the scope and variety of their undertakings. The set of chisels need not be a large one — from 12 to 20 tools will suffice if the shapes are well chosen.

Carving tools are designated by number as well as by size. This system of numbering has been standardized and is used by all manufacturers of wood-carving tools (Fig. 2). Tools having the same relative degree of curvature are given the same number regardless of size. Thus a No. 9 gouge, which has a generally semicircular cutting edge, may range in width from $\frac{1}{16}$ in. the narrowest, to $1\frac{1}{2}$ in. about the widest that is made. Thus the print of the curve made in a piece of wood by the cutting edge of a ¾ in. No. 9 gouge would be a semicircle having a ⅜-in. radius.

Carving tools are formed in various shapes, each shape designed to do a particular kind of cutting (Fig. 3). In addition to tools having straight blades, the carver may select chisels having blades gently curved from cutting edge to handle, or still others in which the blades have been formed to much sharper curves. The former are long-bent or curved chisels, while the latter are short-bent chisels, also sometimes called "spoons." Short-bent gouges are either front-bent or back-bent.

In addition to chisels and gouges, there are parting tools, which are V shaped, and macaroni tools, the cutting edges of which are formed to a square U shape. Then there are spade, or fishtail chisels and gouges, used mostly for putting on the finishing touches, or for light cutting.

The Chisel

First is the chisel, the cutting edge of which is straight (A, Fig. 3). Blades of wood-carving chisels are not as thick

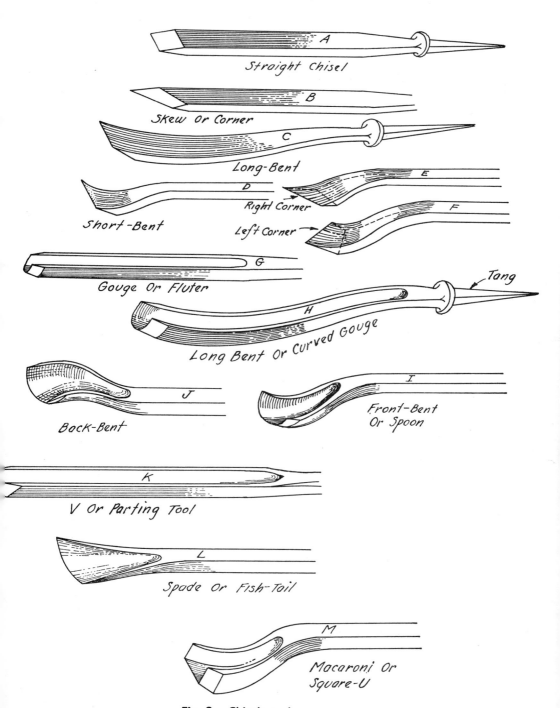

Fig. 3. Chisels and gouges.

A — Straight Chisel
B — Skew Or Corner
C — Long-Bent
D — Short-Bent
E — Right Corner
F — Left Corner
G — Gouge Or Fluter
H — Long Bent Or Curved Gouge
Tang
J — Back-Bent
I — Front-Bent Or Spoon
K — V Or Parting Tool
L — Spade Or Fish-Tail
M — Macaroni Or Square-U

as blades on ordinary woodworker's chisels, nor is the edge sharpened in the same manner. Whereas the ordinary woodworker's chisel has the edge beveled on only one of its sides, the cutting edges of wood-carving chisels are beveled on both sides of the blade. Corner chisels are made by grinding the cutting edge of the straight chisel on an angle (*B*, Fig. 3).

Straight chisels are used for cutting or trimming straight lines, edges, and grooves; for trimming or truing up corners; and for flattening backgrounds.

In addition to chisels having a straight shaft, there are curved (long-bent) chisels, like the one at *C*, and short-bent (spoons) shown at *D*. On short-bent chisels, cutting edges are sharpened either at right angles to the shaft, or for a right corner (*E*), or a left corner (*F*).

Gouges

Gouges, like chisels, are made with shafts straight, curved, or bent. They are available in a variety of sweeps as shown in the chart (Fig. 2) numbers 3 to 11. Gouges with a very shallow sweep are sometimes called extra flats. A very deep gouge is sometimes called a fluter, or a fluting tool, but if it is a very narrow deep gouge, it is then known as a veiner, or a veining tool. A No. 12 long-bent, or curved gouge, has the same sweep as a No. 3 gouge with a straight shaft. A spoon having this same sweep is No. 24, while a back-bent tool having this sweep is No. 33. The chart in Figure 2 will make this system of numbering clear as it relates to the sweep and size of each chisel.

Gouges with straight shafts are the tools most frequently used by the wood-carver, being the workhorses of his kit. They are designed for heavy cutting. Curved gouges are used to remove wood from places which cannot readily be reached with a straight gouge, such as would occur if one were carving a concave surface.

Bent Chisels and Gouges

For removing backgrounds, especially background areas confined in close places between other parts of the carved design, no other tool is so well adapted as the short-bent chisel or gouge. Short-bent tools are also good for many kinds of undercutting. They will reach into corners and tight places which would be inaccessible to a straight, or even a long-bent tool. Cutting edges of bent chisels are ground three different ways: straight across, as at *D* in Figure 3; as at *E*, to make a right-corner tool; or a left-corner tool as at *F*. The corner tools are ground to 45 degrees, or an even sharper angle, to permit working in corners more acute than a right angle.

Front-bent gouges, like the one shown at *I*, are useful when carving work which curves sharply, especially if such work has concave surfaces like those found on a Chippendale claw-and-ball foot. Back-bent gouges are less frequently used than other types, but for special jobs, such as cutting ball-and-claw feet on a Chippendale chair, one or more such tools will prove quite useful.

V Tools

V tools, shown at *K*, and more commonly referred to as parting tools, are the tools most generally used when the work is started for outlining the design preparatory to removing the background. V tools are also used for very fine veining, such as may be found on a leaf. Tools having angles of 90 degrees (No. 39), 65 degrees (No. 40), and 45 degrees (No. 41) may be bought. They are available in straight, long-bent, or short-bent forms.

Spade Tools

Spade gouges, like the one shown at L, and often referred to as fishtail gouges, are used mostly for light cutting, or delicate finishing operations. They are seldom hammered with a mallet, but rather are pushed, or nudged along with the palm of the hand.

Macaroni Tools

The macaroni tool, shown at M, is a square U-shaped tool. The sides of the U are not very high. It is usually a short-bent tool, though occasionally long-bent. It is useful for cutting or trimming grooves, or for working or trimming along a shoulder. It often proves useful for flattening backgrounds.

Background Punches

Though infrequently used by professional wood-carvers, background punches (Fig. 4) and a variety of other stamping tools which make patterns like a star or a leaf are available to the wood-carver. Experienced craftsmen nearly always prefer to trim and smooth their backgrounds very carefully with chisels. When they want a more distinctive background, they

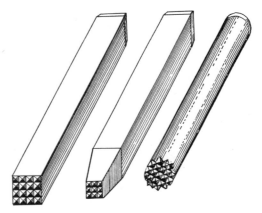

Fig. 4. Carver's background punches.

usually prefer some other means of achieving it than by using stamping tools; such as cutting a diaper pattern, or mottling the background with shallow gouge cuts. There are times, however, when the use of a background punch is justifiable, throwing the raised part of the design into sharper focus. They should be used sparingly, however, and especially so if the design has considerable modeling. They are more suitable for backgrounds on which the surface of the design has been left flat.

Files and Rasps

Small, specially designed woodcarver's rasps are sometimes used, though very sparingly, by the woodcarver. Blades at both ends of the handle, shaped in a variety of ways (Fig. 5) and usually curved, make

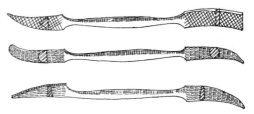

Fig. 5. Wood-carver's rasps.

11

Fig. 6. A mallet.

made of hardwood, preferably hard maple, or close-grained white oak. Lignum vitae, an extremely hard, tough, and heavy wood, is excellent material for a mallet, if it is available. The mallet should be bell-shaped, from 3 in. to 3½ in. in diameter at the bottom, with a well-shaped handle having a diameter of about 1¼ in. Such a mallet is shown in Figure 6.

Jigs

The wood-carver will find it advantageous to resort to using jigs of one kind or another occasionally. Suggestions for making two such jigs, and the uses to which they can be put are shown in Figures 7 and 8. Stock which is to be carved after it has been turned on a lathe is usually difficult to hold in a vise, since there is considerable danger of damaging the sur-

these files and rasps useful tools for cleaning up places which are difficult to reach with a cutting tool.

The Wood-Carver's Mallet

The proper type of mallet is essential to do good work. It should be

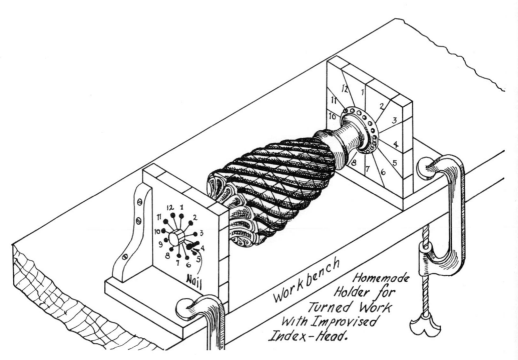

Fig. 7. A jig for turning work.

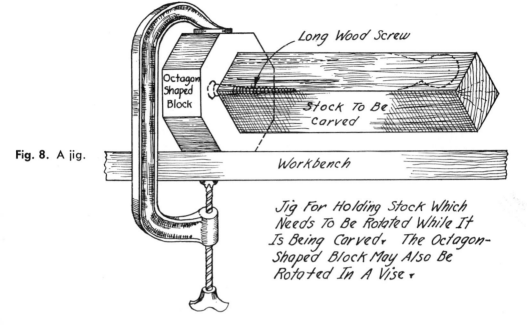

Fig. 8. A jig.

Long Wood Screw

Octagon Shaped Block

Stock To Be Carved

Workbench

Jig For Holding Stock Which Needs To Be Rotated While It Is Being Carved. The Octagon-Shaped Block May Also Be Rotated In A Vise.

face. The turned member also needs to be rotated, not only to carve it, but before carving is begun to lay out the design on its surface. The improvised homemade jig (Fig. 7) in this case provided with an index head, the holes of which are spaced for 30-degree turns, will prove quite useful for making layouts on the surface of the shaft, leg, or column, and for holding or rotating the work while it is being carved. A single hole is all that needs to be drilled into the top of the turning. This will accommodate the nail which keeps the work from rotating while it is being carved.

Still another useful jig is shown in Figure 8. Stock to be carved in the round, such as the figure of a person, must be rotated frequently, or even held at various angles toward or away from the person carving it. By fastening the stock with a heavy screw, or by gluing it to an octagon-shaped block, it may be rotated, or held on top of the workbench with a clamp, or it may be held or rotated in a vise should this prove to be more convenient.

Clamps

Clamps of various kinds, but especially C clamps of various sizes, like the one shown in Figure 9, will be needed to hold work while it is being carved.

Fig. 9. A C clamp.

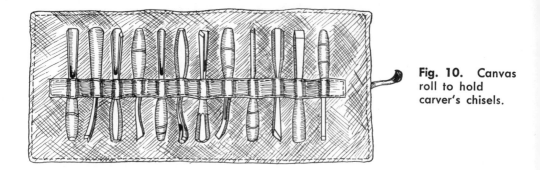

Fig. 10. Canvas roll to hold carver's chisels.

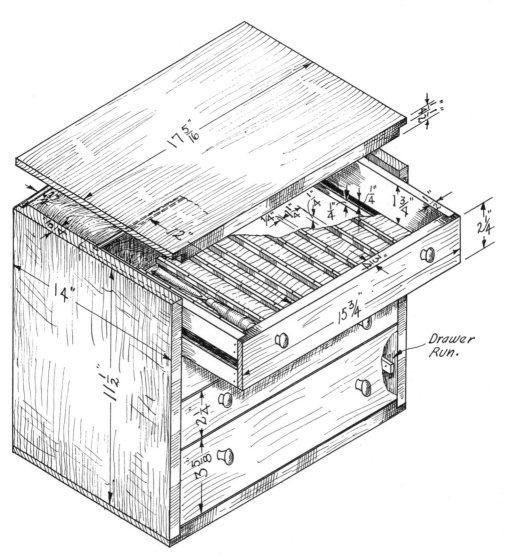

Fig. 11. Cabinet with drawers to hold wood-carving tools.

Tool Storage

Two methods of storing tools so they may be kept in good condition, and at the same time be readily available for use, are shown in Figures 10 and 11. Canvas rolls, made wide enough to fold over the tools at both ends, may be neatly rolled and tied for convenient storage of tools and just as easily unrolled and spread out in front of the work when needed.

The small cabinet with drawers (Fig. 11), a worthwhile but somewhat ambitious project, is not only a good storage place for wood-carving tools, but decorating the drawer fronts (Figs. 12 and 13) presents the beginning wood-carver a challenging project. A good wood to use for these drawer fronts is rock maple, but birch, red gum, or poplar are also suitable and will carve well. In the case of red gum or poplar only heartwood is suitable for carving. The sapwood of these trees is either tough, or soft enough to present objectionable handicaps, especially to an inexperienced wood-carver. While the three upper drawers were designed to hold ten chisels apiece, they can be made to hold twice that many if two tools are placed into each compartment. The chisels should be paired so that the blade of one lies next to the handle of its mate to avoid crowding.

The Workbench

One of the most important pieces of equipment the wood-carver can own is his workbench. While one may, of course, carve on the kitchen table if nothing better is available, such

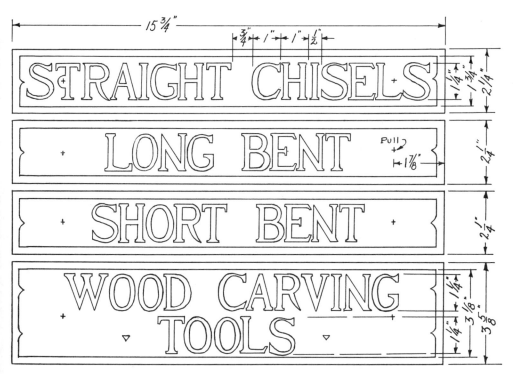

Fig. 12. Layout for carving the front of the carving-tool cabinet.

Fig. 13. Type of carving used on drawer fronts. The background is carved out to a depth of $\frac{1}{16}$ in.

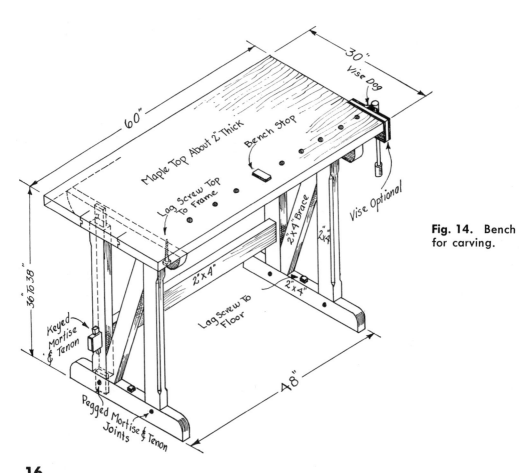

Fig. 14. Bench for carving.

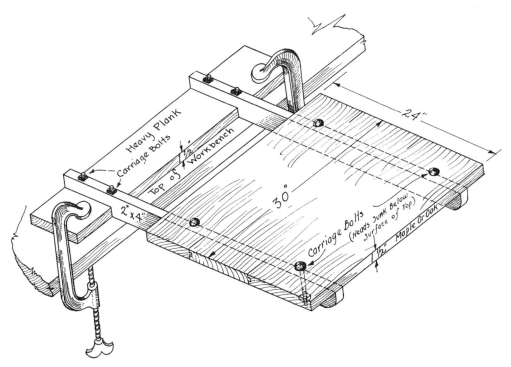

Fig. 15. Carver's table — may be fitted to top of regular workbench.

work stations are not always conducive to comfort or efficiency. For anyone desiring seriously to take up wood carving as a hobby, making a workbench (Fig. 14) would certainly be a worthwhile undertaking. Such a workbench, placed near a window where you have a northern exposure, will provide an ideal work station. The vise at the right end of the table is so useful as to be almost indispensable for holding work in its jaws, or together with a bench stop to hold work on top of the bench.

For the person who already has a good woodworker's bench, a carver's board (Fig. 15) may be clamped to the top of the workbench, thus raising the working surface to a height at which it may be more comfortable to carve.

Sharpening the Tools

It is very important that wood-carving tools be properly sharpened, and kept sharp, if good results are to be achieved. Both knives and chisels must constantly be kept in the finest condition if good work is to be done. For getting a good bevel on the tool, a grinder of some sort is needed. This may be either a hand-operated grinder like the one shown in Figure 16, or a motor-driven grinder like the one shown in Figure 17. The grinder should be equipped with a fine grit aluminum oxide wheel rather than an emery wheel, since aluminum oxide generates less heat and, therefore, does not so easily burn the steel. The direction of rotation of the wheel should be toward the edge of the tool, as shown in Figure 17.

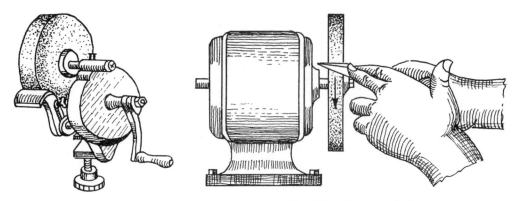

Fig. 16. Hand grinder.   Fig. 17. Power grinder.

When grinding a knife blade, the bevel should be wide, and hollow-ground, as shown in Figure 18 at *B*, rather than narrow and blunt as at *A*. A blade sharpened with a wide bevel cuts easily even on softwood where a short-bevel blade could hardly be made to work at all. Carving chisels likewise, should be ground with a fairly long bevel on the outside of the tool, except occasionally for special types of cutting which call for a shorter bevel.

Wood-carving chisels differ from ordinary woodworker's chisels in that they are almost invariably beveled on

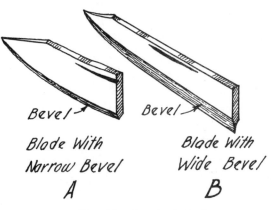

Bevel

Bevel

Blade With
Narrow Bevel

Blade With
Wide Bevel

A   B

Fig. 18. Bevel of blades.

both sides at the cutting edge. This holds true whether the cutting edge is sharpened straight across or at an angle. See *A* and *B*, Figure 3. Gouges and parting tools, while they have the greater bevel on the outside of the chisel, are also very slightly beveled on the inside of the tool. All of the beveling on the inside of the tool is done with the carver's slips. Since this is the case, it takes a lot of patient honing to put a new tool into first-class shape. The inside bevel need not, however, be achieved all at once, nor at the first honing, but will come about gradually as a result of many honings with the oilstone slips. A new tool will do good work if the outside bevel is kept in good condition and the edge kept sharp.

Once the correct bevel has been ground on a gouge or a straight chisel, a knife, parting tool, or what have you, the blades need to be whetted and honed on a fine-grit oilstone. A fine-grit carborundum stone will do very satisfactory work, but for really fine sharpening and a keen edge, the tool should be finished off on a natural Arkansas. Arkansas stones are white,

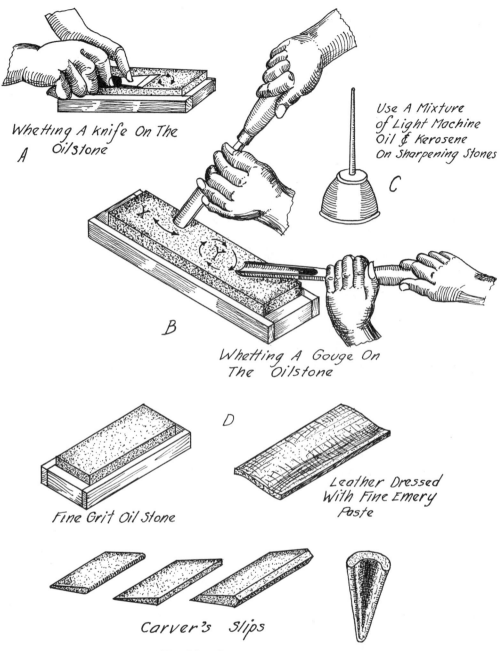

A Whetting A Knife On The Oilstone

C Use A Mixture of Light Machine Oil & Kerosene On Sharpening Stones

B Whetting A Gouge On The Oilstone

D Fine Grit Oil Stone

Leather Dressed With Fine Emery Paste

Carver's Slips

Fig. 19. Sharpening tools.

hard, and have a very fine abrasive surface.

To whet a knife on the oilstone, hold it at a very low angle, raising the handle only slightly higher than the surface of the stone. Then hone it, using a circular, clockwise motion (Fig. 19 at A). Hone against the cutting edge — not away from it. Alternate from one side to the other frequently when whetting, so as to get a keen edge in the shortest possible time.

Gouges are sharpened as shown in Figure 19 at *B*. They are held on the stone at an angle of about 15 degrees, and moved over the stone in a clockwise direction, as shown at *Y*, while the handle is slowly rotated in order to allow every part of the beveled surface to make contact with the surface of the stone. The bevel is honed still smoother by finishing it off with sidewise motions, as shown at *X*, while at the same time rotating the handle to right and left.

The whetting and honing is continued until a burr has been turned up on the inside of the gouge. This burr is then removed with a slipstone.

V tools are the most difficult to sharpen. They must be very carefully ground if both sides of the V are to be kept alike. The bevels on the outside of the tool are sharpened much in the same way as you would sharpen a straight chisel, by raising the tool to an angle of about 15 degrees off the

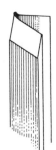

Fig. 21. Point produced by sharpening bevels.

stone, and then rubbing it over the stone with a clockwise, and at times with a back and forward motion, as shown in Figure 20, at *A*. This is continued until burrs are turned up on both cutting edges inside the V. The sharpening process also will cause a sharp corner to form on the bevel where the two sides are joined together. This sharp corner, if not removed, would cause the tool to dig into the wood at too rapid a rate, and also would result in making it difficult to push the tool along in the wood. It is best to round this sharp corner slightly in the manner shown at *B* in Figure 20.

It will also develop that forming the outside bevels will result in a protruding point at the apex of the V (Fig. 21). This protruding point re-

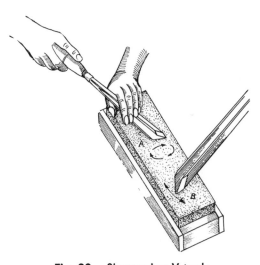

Fig. 20. Sharpening V tools.

Fig. 22. Removing the burr on the inside of a V tool on a slipstone.

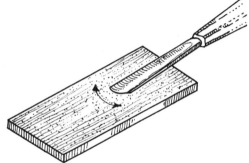

Fig. 23. Stropping the outside bevel of a gouge on leather dressed with emery paste.

Fig. 24. Stropping a chisel on leather.

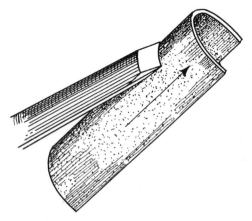

Fig. 25. Stropping the inside of a gouge.

sults from the rounding and, consequently, the thickening of the corner on the inside of the chisel where the two sides are joined. This protruding point also should be removed by honing (*B*, Fig. 20). Any burr left inside the tool should be removed (Fig. 22).

Once the tools have been properly ground and honed, they should be given a final stropping on a piece of leather. Secure a fairly heavy piece of leather about 3 by 6 in., dressing it with oil and very fine emery powder. This makes an excellent stropping tool. Figures 23, 24, and 25 show three ways in which the leather may be used to strop the tool. When it is not in use, keep the leather under cover to prevent grit or dirt from spoiling its surface.

CHAPTER 2   Methods and Techniques

Wood carving may seem to be such a difficult art to master to anyone who has never before attempted it that there is some danger he may be discouraged from trying it. This especially may be the case if, as so often happens, he views an intricately carved object which may have been executed by a master craftsman who has had years of training and experience, and whose workmanship is obviously so flawless that the viewer feels he could never hope to equal it.

Obviously, what the amateur, and especially the beginner must come to realize is that every master craftsman had to undergo a period of training, and that in most instances the initial steps were humble enough. Learning to draw reasonably well is a good first step for the beginner in learning to carve. Some practice at modeling in clay is also desirable. But it is possible to learn to do creditable work in wood carving without becoming proficient in either drawing, or modeling with clay.

Speaking in broad general terms, there are but four different types of wood carving: (1) scratch, or line carving; (2) flat surface carving in low relief; (3) relief carving with design modeled; (4) carving in the round. We have listed these in proper sequence from the easiest to the most difficult. There are, of course, degrees of difficulty under each category.

Scratch, or Line Carving

Scratch, or line carving in its simplest form, consists of little more than cutting narrow and shallow grooves into the wood. The tools used in doing this are either the V tool, or narrow veining or grooving tools; usually the ⅛-in. veiner. There are, however, degrees of difficulty, and degrees of refinement to this simplest type of carving. We may compare it to the practice of penmanship; the ordinary outlining of a design to ordinary strokes of a pen in writing or drawing. The greater refinements of the art reveal themselves through long sweeping cuts of the tool, with gradual widening of the line for emphasis, or gradual narrowing of the line to the point, almost, of invisibility for delicacy and grace. The cutting though, in either case, must be crisp and clean. Surface texture in the more intricate designs may be achieved by cutting a series of lines to form a pattern over parts of the surface. The Japanese do scratch carving rather well, often achieving a meaningful design with a minimum number of strokes or cuts.

The girl at the well (Fig. 78) is an example of the simple type of scratch carving, in which elements of the design are merely outlined, the cuts used being all about alike. The wheat design (Fig. 77) comparatively simple though it is, has elements of greater refinement. The same is true of the designs found on the spoon rack (Fig. 72). In the spoon rack, moreover, some surface texture may be added to parts of the design, either by a series of fine parallel lines cut with a V tool, or by cross-hatching V-tool lines on the background of the design elements that were shaded.

Fig. 26. Driving a chisel with a mallet.

Scratch carving techniques are carried over into the three other types of carving, and used there to achieve surface decoration and texture, as on the carving of the bear, for example.

To make this type of carving look well, it is necessary to have the cutting edges of the tools very sharp, so that clean cuts across the grain, as well as with the grain, are possible. An experienced wood-carver will cut away or toward himself with equal facility.

The easiest method of controlling the chisels in doing this kind of carving is to grip the blade of the chisel, or the lower part of the handle, firmly, while driving the chisel through the wood with light taps of the wood-carver's mallet. This method makes it easy to maneuver the tool around curves and corners, and results in fairly good control of both length and depth of cut. This method of driving the chisel is shown in Figure 26.

Greater skill is required if the chisel used is pushed along with the palm of the hand. A right-handed person will grip the top of the blade or lower end of the handle with his left hand, which also guides and controls the sweep of the tool, while using the

palm of the right hand to push the tool through the wood. This method of using the chisel is shown in Figure 27.

When the chisel is being pushed along the lines being cut (Fig. 27), it is held steady, but firm down against and into the wood with the forward hand, and at the same time pushed forward with the hand holding the handle. This method of cutting works rather well on the long sweeps, where lines do not change direction too sud-

Fig. 27. Driving a chisel by hand.

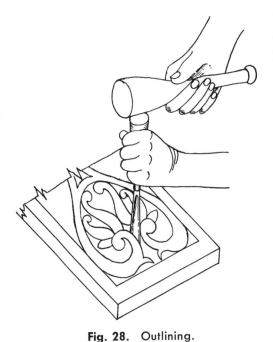

Fig. 28. Outlining.

Examples of this kind of wood carving are the bookstall (Fig. 94) and the fireplace bellows (Fig. 89).

To do flat surface carving in low relief, first draw the design directly on the wood freehand, or transfer it to the wood from tracing paper, on which the design has first been drawn with a soft lead pencil. It is better not to use carbon paper for this purpose if any other way can be found to transfer a design to the wood, because carbon paper lines smudge or blur easily. Sharp, clear lines to go by in outlining the work with carving tools are desirable. Any lines not sharp or true on the wood should be corrected before any cutting or carving is started.

Once the design has been satisfactorily drawn or transferred to the surface to be carved, the design must be outlined with carving chisels or a sharp knife. Professional wood-carvers do not use a knife to cut outlines, or at least the author has never seen one do so, but in doing his own carving he finds this method of cutting outlines very satisfactory at times. Professional wood-carvers outline every part of a design (Fig. 28) by driving the chisel straight down into the wood with a mallet. To be sure, the first cuts in outlining a design should not be driven deeply into the wood, since to do so might loosen or chip away parts of the surface of the design which the wood-carver does not wish to remove. So, easy does it, when first outlining the design preparatory to removing background waste. This holds true also when outlining work which is to be modeled in relief, though in this case some remedial work is usually possible

denly. When lines curve more quickly it is easier to wiggle the tool ever so slightly from side to side as it is being pushed along. This not only facilitates the cutting but helps to keep the tool from taking a wrong direction. On some of the softwoods it is almost impossible to make a clean cut across the grain using a V tool or a veining tool; and the method of outlining shown in Figure 28 must then be used.

Level Surface Carving in Low Relief

Level surface carving in low relief is a little more difficult to do than scratch carving, because in this type of carving the work is carried a step or two farther. The desired effect is achieved by lowering background areas surrounding or adjoining the design proper, thereby in effect raising the design proper, and throwing it into relief against this lowered background.

if pieces are inadvertently chipped off.

Before telling how background waste is removed in doing level surface carving, we want to explore a bit more thoroughly the methods and techniques of outlining the design. Professional wood-carvers are trained to carve with chisels exclusively; and, therefore, seldom, if ever, use knives to do any part of their work. The first carving the author ever did was done with a sloyd knife, and having done quite a lot of whittling with knives since then, he has found the knife to be a versatile and useful adjunct to his wood-carving kit. Moreover, whereas most professional wood-carvers have a rather large assortment of chisels with a wide variety of curves and widths, most amateurs may not be so well equipped. The best substitute tool to use in overcoming this deficiency, especially when outlining a design, is a good sharp-pointed sloyd knife (Fig. 1).

Such a knife is particularly well adapted for cutting into sharp corners where chisels, especially in unskilled hands, might chip away parts of the design one wishes to keep. So, do not despise the knife or refrain from using it where it may be used to good advantage.

Most parts of a level surface design may be effectively outlined with sharp chisels, using the widest variety of sweeps and widths available. Do this part of outlining by driving the tool straight down into the wood fairly close to the pencil lines, cutting, of course, a little on the outside of the lines on the waste side. One should never cut exactly to the outline of a design before the full depth of background areas has been reached. Only after the background areas have been carefully leveled off, and tooled, should outlines be chiseled exactly to the true line. This final cutting should be very carefully done with crisp, clean cuts using very sharp chisels.

A third method of outlining a design, or parts of it, is the same one that is used in doing scratch or line carving. Use either a narrow V tool, or a U-shaped veiner where the outline is long and regular.

Once the design has been outlined, it is ready to have the waste wood in the background areas removed to whatever depth has been decided upon. This depth will depend upon the style and character of the design, and to some extent upon the type of wood being carved. For large-scale designs, let us say, in oak, the background areas of which are also large, deep cuts of $\frac{1}{4}$ in. or more may be made. Where the scale of the design is smaller, and where the finer grained woods, such as California sugar pine, or mahogany are used, backgrounds often are cut no more than $\frac{1}{16}$ in. deep.

When starting to remove this background, it is best, once the design has been outlined with cuts all around, to make short, rather sharp-angled cuts from pretty close to the outline, rather than long-angled cuts from a greater distance. This prevents cutting into the design inadvertently, since the momentum of the tool is not so greatly accelerated making the shorter cuts, and the tool is, as a result, more easily controlled.

Once this wood in the background immediately surrounding the outline of the design has been removed, the balance of these areas may be cut to proper depth with longer sweeps of the chisel, with far less danger that the chisel may slip and chip away parts of the design.

The tools which should be used to remove background areas are extra flats mostly No. 3 and No. 4 sweeps of various widths. These are better suited to tooling a background than a straight chisel would be, since they will not dig at the corners, but at the same time are flat enough to give it that well-tooled, but not mechanically perfect, look which is a feature of all good wood carving.

Both square U macaroni tools, and wide-angled V tools, as well as curved chisels of all shapes, may be used to true up at the edges of a design when putting on the finishing touches. Backgrounds which have been cut to their proper depth should have most of the finishing cuts going in the same, or about the same, direction rather than haphazardly in every direction, for the most pleasing effect.

Finally a word or two about sandpapering. The work of the highly skilled craftsman needs very little, if any, sanding. Much of the best work is not sanded at all. However, in most instances some sanding is necessary, especially before a high degree of skill has been acquired. Make it a rule to do no sandpapering until no more cutting with edge tools needs to be done, since the abrasive material left by sandpaper on the wood quickly dulls the keenest edge on a chisel and prevents one from doing satisfactory work with it.

When sanding, use only very fine-grit abrasives, with flexible paper back, such as 6/0 or 8/0 open coat garnet papers. Avoid sanding across the grain as much as possible, to prevent scratches, which show up badly under any kind of finish.

Carving in Low Relief
With Modeling

Carving in low relief with modeling merely carries level surface carving a step farther by shaping, rounding, or otherwise modeling the surfaces of the design elements and areas being carved. An example would be carving a leaf and not only outlining its shape, but raising or lowering adjacent areas to give form and contour to its surface. This type of carving is that found on the better types of period furniture and other smaller objects found in this book. While this description seems disarmingly simple, actual accomplishment of the fact is not always simple.

Take a leaf, for example. There are many different kinds of leaves to choose from. Leaves whose outlines are fairly regular, like the one shown in Figure 29, would be rather easy to carve. Its outline is regular, it is easy to draw, and easy to outline with carving tools. Modeling its surface will not prove to be extremely difficult. Such leaves appear on the frame of the serving tray (Fig. 100), and are a good simple type for the beginner to carve.

There are, however, a great variety of leaf types, many of which are not so simple when it comes to carving a good likeness. Chief among these is the acanthus leaf, an example of which appears on the Madonna shrine wall bracket (Fig. 54). Wood-carvers for centuries have delighted in using their ingenuity to find new ways to reveal

Fig. 29. Leaf.

the beauty of its sinuous curves, undulations, and indentations, with the result that the variety of forms in which it has been carved are almost beyond description.

In describing tool techniques and carving methods for doing this type of carving, we shall refer to the bookends (Fig. 125). First, the block of wood must be shaped and formed (Fig. 126) and the design drawn thereon.

Outline the design with chisel cuts, choosing chisels with curvatures or sweeps corresponding as nearly as possible to the part of the outline you are cutting. Hammer the chisel straight down into the wood with the mallet, but do not cut deep. Stay at least $\frac{1}{16}$ in. away from the lines you have drawn when doing this. If your kit of chisels does not include all the sweeps and sizes you need, it is possible to adapt the flatter sweeps to sharper curves by tilting the chisel slightly and driving only the corner of the cutting edge into the wood.

For longer unbroken curves, such as those found on the right side of the leaf, or near the bottom, a long-bent V tool will do the trick. The V tool is also the best tool to use in outlining the long riblike leaf veins when doing the modeling on the leaf. Do no modeling on the leaf surface

at this time, but wait until some or all of the background areas have been cut to their proper depth, which on this carving is about $\frac{3}{16}$ in. Do, however, outline the part of the leaf near the bottom of the carving which overlaps other parts of the leaf.

Now make short, high-angle chisel cuts, cutting from the direction of the background areas toward the ones you made when you outlined the design. Continue making cuts at lower angles until background areas have been lowered to their full depth. With extra flats, smooth these areas. Then trim all outlines exactly to the line, cutting clean, and without leaving tool-cut marks where outline and background meet. It is very important to get clean, sharp outlines, and the good craftsman will not be satisfied to do otherwise.

To begin modeling the leaf, outline the veins, and outline the areas which are to be beaded. These beads, which represent droplets of water on the leaf, have the pods in which they lay cut nearly as deep as the background areas surrounding the leaf. Next cut around each bead, using a chisel having the curve of a half circle. Trim out the background waste at the same time you round the beads with a straight $\frac{1}{8}$-in. chisel, the cutting edge of which is beveled on both sides, as should be the case with the cutting edges of all straight wood-carving chisels. A $\frac{1}{4}$-in. skew, and a narrow extra flat may also be used for doing this rounding over of the beads.

Modeling the rest of the leaf is largely a matter of using your own judgment, so far as giving it just the shape you want is concerned. In order to bring the veins up, the areas sur-

27

rounding them must be lowered sufficiently until they can be properly rounded over on top, and this rounding is done with the heel of the skew. Some edges of the leaf are left high, level, or nearly level with the original surface. Other edges are rounded down. Modeling on other parts is left largely to the judgment, skill, and whims of the individual who does the carving, which after all is what gives handwork individuality and character. Carelessness in making the finishing cuts will show, and tool marks that the wood-carver intends to leave on the work must be tooled in with precision and care.

A word more about techniques of handling the chisels on which to close our instructions for doing modeled low-relief carving. The skilled wood-carver cuts with equal facility in almost any direction without moving or turning about the carving itself. In the beginning the novice will have some difficulty getting accustomed to this, but when he sees advantages gained by doing it that way, such as time saved, he will soon get used to it. He may have split-offs or chipping because of unexpected changes in the direction of the grain, or from not being familiar with how the grain of certain types of wood behaves as the cutting is directed elsewhere. It will not be long, however, before he will sense these changes in the direction of the grain, and will adjust to them almost automatically until few if any such accidents will occur. Hold sanding to a mimimum, doing just enough to clean rough spots impossible to smooth with the chisels. Marks of the tool denote hand carving, but the more

nearly smooth and uniform they leave the surface, the more satisfying the results will be.

Carving in the Round and Whittling

Carving in the round entails many of the techniques and skills used in doing the types of carving just described. In many respects it is quite different, however, because the object is three-dimensional instead of two. Carving in the round involves knowing the shape of things, and in carving figures found in the animal world, or human figures, two categories into which most of this type of carving falls. Some knowledge of anatomy is essential. One can become sufficiently well acquainted with essential features of most animals, and human beings, so one may reproduce satisfactory likenesses without getting too technically involved in a study of bone and muscle structure, useful as these might be, by the mere process of careful observation.

Since most of the figures to be carved in the round shown in the book are small, they may be carved almost entirely with sharp pocketknives. Very large objects, such as heads, or busts carved in proportions almost lifelike will need to be done with chisels, since knives would not work nearly so well. But where an object to be carved in the round may easily be held in the hand, a good pocketknife is easily the better tool to do the greater part of the carving.

While it is possible to carve pieces like the horse, the bear, or the dog, all shown in the book, from squared blocks of the proper sizes, with no preliminary shaping except what a pocketknife will do, the more sensible thing is first to saw the block to its rough shape on a band saw, jig saw, or by using a coping saw if these power tools are not available (Fig. 43).

A fairly large blade will be required for heavy cutting, or boasting-in the carving. By boasting-in we mean the rough, preliminary cutting which must be done to achieve the rough form of the figure.

When boasting-in a carving with a knife, the wood-carver cuts both toward and away from himself, the direction of the cut depending upon the direction of the grain, and the ease with which the chips may be removed by cutting in that particular direction. A precaution to be kept in mind at all times is to keep fingers well below the sweep of the cutting edge of the blade just in case it should slip.

On animal carvings like "Question Mark," boasting-in consists of cutting away excess stock between and around legs, and roughly rounding the long neck and body. Some carvings are left in this rough-cut effect. The long-eared hound falls into this category, since one of the features of this carving is the broad facets left by heavy cutting and wide sweeps of the blade. This does not denote carelessness in cutting, but is an effect deliberately planned that way from the beginning (Fig. 44). Even on this carving many of the finishing touches must be done with a small-bladed knife, especially many of those on the underside of his body, and around his head, such as eyes and nose.

Other carvings, like the horse (Fig. 39) are carefully detailed to register the minutest details, such as hairlines, muscle and bone structure, and similar fine details. In the carving of the bear, a lot of attention is paid to surface texture to get the desired effect, and in this case these lines and details are chiseled in with a fine veining tool.

For smoothing rough contours, left by boasting-in cuts, a clip blade (Fig. 1) works well. Finer details, such as eyes and fine hairlines may be finished off with a tiny pen blade, which is short, thin, and has a very fine point.

While it may seem unimportant to exercise any particular care during the boasting-in stage, it is advisable to do so, in order not to lose the essential form or shape of the object. When this part of the operation has been completed, what is left to do should merely consist of putting in the refining touches which bring out those features that distinguish the work of the individual craftsman, or delineate features he wishes to emphasize.

The types of blades preferred by various wood-carvers will vary, since everyone who carves will become attached to one type or another in the course of time. The skew-edged blade (Fig. 1), for example, will serve to do all of the delicate cutting for which the thin, slender pen blade is intended, though some may prefer to use the latter. The skew blade is best adapted to do chip carving if a knife is used, and this type of knife has a fixed blade, a safety feature not to be overlooked.

Carving in the round, since few straight edges, or lines are prevalent in such figures, requires working from center lines, or designated points on a surface. Drawing and locating these on various parts of the work as early as possible is important, in order to get a true and accurate representation of a likeness. Such lines and check points should be located on the blank whenever possible right after sawing it to its rough shape. Such lines and check points must be re-drawn, adjusted, or re-located as often as this becomes necessary as work on the carving progresses.

Chisels should be used even on the smallest carvings whenever any advantage may be gained by doing so. Often in close places, such as narrow openings between ears, or where legs are joined to the body, or for deep undercutting, chisels will do a better job than a knife.

To sandpaper a figure carved in the round, we give practically the same instructions as we did for sanding other types of carving; viz., do as little sanding as possible. For much of the sanding that has to be done it is best to cut sandpaper into long narrow strips about an inch or less in width, and then carefully fold it lengthwise so the abrasive surface is exposed on both sides. This strip of sandpaper, lightly rubbed over the surface, especially in areas not accessible to a larger piece of sandpaper, will do the job. Where surfaces are rounded, especially concave areas, it is best to form sandpaper into a roll to fit the place where it is to be used. Use 6/0 or 8/0 garnet paper.

CHAPTER 3 How to Draw Designs and Patterns

In this book, as many of the carving designs and patterns as possible have been reproduced full-size for the convenience of those who wish to use them. In a number of instances, however, where the size of the object to be carved is greater than the page size of the book, it has been impractical to reproduce full-size patterns. We shall cover briefly, therefore, the process of making full-sized patterns from reproductions which have been reduced in size.

Patterns and designs for the projects which have been drawn at a scale larger than can be accommodated by the page size have graph squares drawn over them. An example of this is Figure 36, page 34. The size at which these graph squares must be drawn to reproduce the design full-size is then given. In Figure 36 they are ½-in. squares. This means that a sheet of paper or cardboard 4½ in. wide and 7 in. long must be filled with graph squares measuring ½ by ½ in. The points through which the lines which make up the design are to be drawn may then be located and put on the pattern at full scale.

To make the locating of these points as easy as possible, each vertical line and each horizontal line is given a number or is designated with a letter of the alphabet. If the person wishing

to reproduce a particular pattern will duplicate these numbers or letters on the drawing he makes, the job will be simplified. On the pattern shown in Figure 78, for example, it will be noticed that the tree foliage curves in at the intersection of second vertical line from the left and the fifth horizontal line from the top. Mark similar points where the foliage curves in. Then connect these points with smooth curves. Other curved surfaces are drawn in a similar way by marking where they cross the horizontal and vertical lines and then connecting these points with smooth curves.

It is true, many of the points will fall at places which cannot be determined to the exact 64ths of an inch. On a pattern with a great many lines, it is best not to try to locate all points before drawing the design. Try first to locate the more important elements, such as centers and radii of circles; then draw the circles. Then fill in with minor elements. Try to judge as accurately as you know how where points must be located in order to draw lines of the design through them and in order to reproduce the design accurately at full size.

Since full-size drawings of a design may be reproduced by this method, it follows naturally that it will also be possible to reproduce accurate patterns at a smaller or a larger scale simply by reducing or enlarging the graph squares upon which the pattern is drawn. Thus, should it be desired to carve a project only three fourths as large as suggested, the graph squares would be drawn ¾ in. square instead of 1 in. square.

Once a design has been drawn on paper, there is always the problem of how best to transfer it to the wood for carving. If the surface upon which the design is to be drawn is flat, and only one carving of a particular design is to be made, it may be drawn on a piece of tracing paper with soft lead pencil, and then transferred directly to the wood from the tracing paper by going over the lines of the tracing on the opposite side with a hard lead pencil. This may be done where the pattern will remain the same if the paper is turned over, as is the case where a design like Figure 76 on page 69 is to be reproduced. Since the left side of the design is a duplicate of the right side, turning the paper over to trace the design upon the wood will not change the pattern. There are instances, however, where turning the paper would turn the design in reverse (Fig. 127) that is, the leaf would be turned in the opposite direction when traced from the opposite side. In these cases it is first necessary to retrace the drawing on the reverse side of the paper, transferring this image from the paper to the wood. An alternative is to use carbon paper under the first tracing.

Truing up of the design will in most instances be necessary after it has been transferred to the wood and before carving it begun. The more accurately

Fig. 30. The shaded parts of the stencil are cut out.

the drawing is made the easier it is to do the carving. In many instances only the main outlines can be drawn to start the carving, and other details must be drawn in as they are needed after certain parts have been carved.

Most professional wood-carvers cut a stencil of any pattern which they must reproduce more than once. A stencil may be cut from ordinary drawing paper if it is not to be used too many times. Cardboard or pressboard is more durable if it is to be used a number of times. If the pattern is to be drawn on a curved or modeled surface, it must also be flexible.

To make a stencil of the bookstall end (Fig. 94) merely draw the design on paper or cardboard and cut out the shaded background portions with a sharp knife. Many wood-carvers prefer to cut their stencils with carving chisels. The design of a pattern like Figure 94 would remain in place with the background areas removed. But some designs (Fig. 128) have lines close together and so placed that the design would not stay in place if the usual stencil were used. For these, use a stencil laid out as shown in Figure 30.

32

Bear

Carving this bear is something of a challenge. His pose is intriguing because of the angle and tilt of his head. The photograph (Fig. 34) shows him to be quite an interesting and somewhat extraordinary subject. His shaggy coat, so realistically reproduced here, is the result of very carefully planned and carefully executed strokes with veining and fluting tools.

Patterns to trace on wood prepara-

Fig. 34.   The bear.

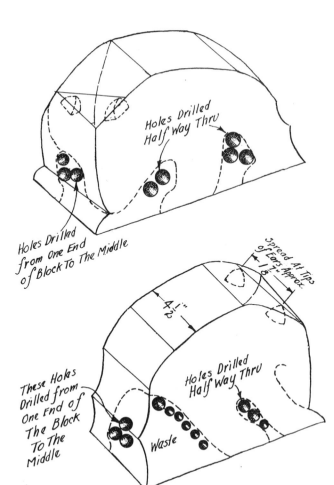

Fig. 35.   Cutting out the blanks.

Holes Drilled Half Way Thru

Holes Drilled from One End of Block To The Middle

These Holes Drilled from One End of The Block To The Middle

Waste

Holes Drilled Half Way Thru

Spread At Tips of Ears Approx. 1 3/8

4 1/2"

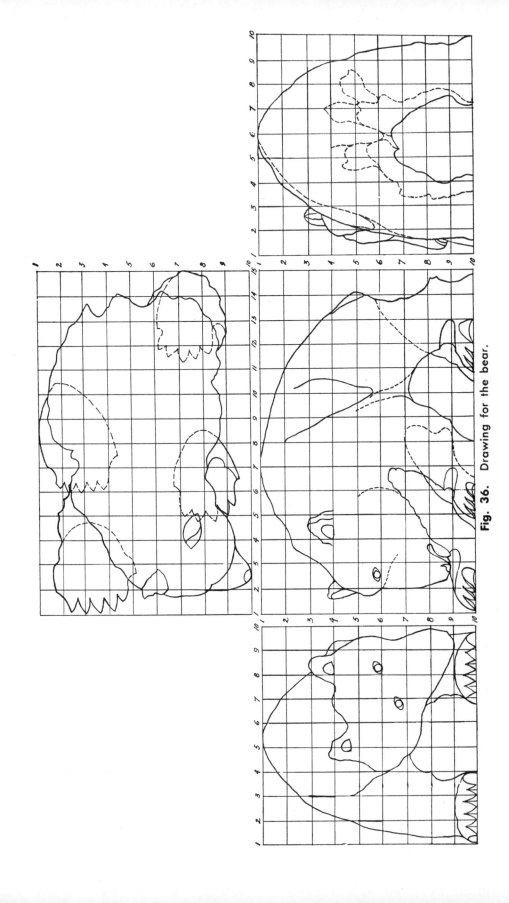

Fig. 36. Drawing for the bear.

Fig. 37. Left-side view of the bear.

tory to cutting a blank from which to carve the bear, may be made from the drawing (Fig. 36). The cutout blanks will appear as those in Figure 35. These two illustrations also show how, by first drilling holes, it will be easier to remove the waste wood underneath his body.

Next shape his body (Fig. 38). Cut deep grooves between head and shoulders, between the upper parts of his legs on both sides of his body, and on both sides of what represents a tail of sorts. Then shape the rest of his body, and his head. The ridge

made by his spine is rather sharp.

Shape his feet, and the underside of his head and belly next. Carefully finish up this portion of his body, which should include the insides of all four legs, with narrow gouges and veining tools. Since less care need be taken here than when carving him topside, this area will afford good practice for the more careful finishing cuts to be made on his shaggy coat later. The drawing shows the type of cutting to be used on the insides of his legs (Fig. 37).

When making the gouge and veiner cuts on the outside of his body, pay particular attention to the pattern formed by these cuts.

The bear's nose is fairly smooth on top. His eyes are two small shiny black beads set into drilled sockets. The ears are small and are, possibly, his least attractive feature.

White pine, if stained a Van Dyke brown, will give the proper coloring. Black walnut, a much harder, much better material to use, may be fiinshed with nothing more than wax to secure the proper color and finish.

Fig. 38. Right-side view of the bear.

Stepping Horse

Anyone who really loves animals, and horses especially, should love to carve the stepping horse (Figs. 39–41). If close attention is paid to details, such as muscle and bone contour, one should achieve an excellent carving. The horse may be made as large as desired, by enlarging the ¼ in. graph squares (Fig. 42), and then drawing the pattern at a larger scale than the one called for here.

Mahogany is a good material to use in carving this horse. A piece 1½ in. thick by 4 in. wide by 4¼ in. high will be needed to carve the horse as shown. This does not include the base, which may be made and carved separately. The horse is then glued to it. The carving is more easily done if it is put together this way. There is no other reason, however, why the horse and its base may not be carved from a single piece of wood, if one wants to go to the trouble. The grain should run vertically on the horse. On the base it runs horizontally.

If the horse is carved without the base, most of the waste may be removed on a band saw. A coping saw may also be used, if this part must be done by hand. Should it be de-cided to make the base a part of the horse when it is carved, holes should be drilled through the waste parts, after which a jig saw or a coping saw may be used to saw out the rest of it.

The closer one can saw to the actual outline without crossing it, the easier it will be to carve afterward. Most of the preliminary cutting will consist of rounding sharp corners which remain after the sawing. Putting on the finishing touches is a more delicate and exacting task. Careful cutting and trimming are necessary to achieve the detail shown on our drawings.

Most of the carving on the horse is done more easily with a sharp pocketknife. Places at the tops of the legs on the inside may be cut out more easily with gouges. Gouges should be used to carve the top of the base. His mane and his tail, which may look difficult to do, actually are not hard to carve. Outline each tuft or strand, and round them over afterward. If care is taken to do the outlining properly, the subsequent shaping is simple. Eyes always require careful cutting, especially when they are small as they will be on a figure this size. Outline the eyeball with the

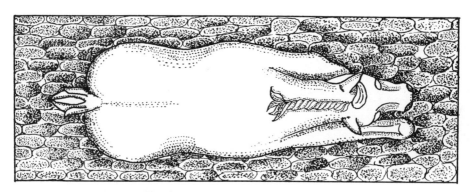

Fig. 39. Top view of the horse.

point of a very sharp penknife blade. Trim to shape very carefully.

If mahogany was used, nothing more than wax need be applied as a finish. A darker, richer hue will result if boiled linseed oil is first rubbed into the wood, followed by wax after it has dried. Repeated coats of oil, vigorously polished and rubbed, will also give an excellent finish.

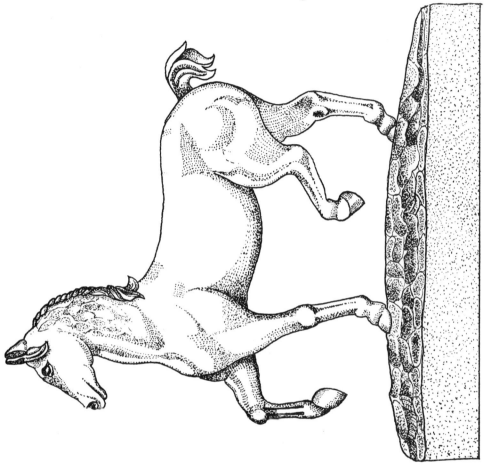

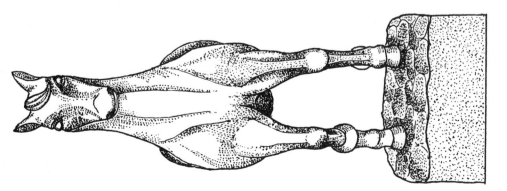

Fig. 40. Front and left-side views of the horse.

37

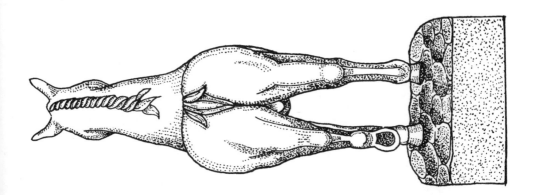

Fig. 41. Rear and right-side view of the horse.

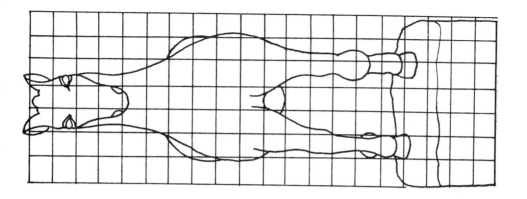

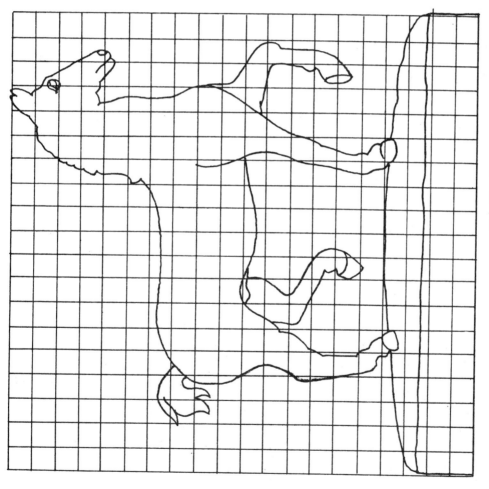

Fig. 42. Pattern for the stepping horse.

Long-Eared Hound

A very interesting carving, and one not too difficult to do, is the long-eared hound (Figs. 43 and 44). Mrs. Amanda Watkins Hellum, coauthor of an earlier wood-carving book by the author, designed this piece.

It is easier to whittle a figure like this with a good sharp knife than with wood-carving chisels, because by using a knife, the figure may be held in one hand and readily moved about to various positions to facilitate the work.

A pattern from which the blank may be cut is shown full size (Fig. 45). On this pattern, lines for cutting the numerous facets found all over the hound's body are also shown. It should be noted here that these need not necessarily be followed exactly when reproducing the carving, but they should serve as a guide in planning the various cuts that have to be made. If the carving is to be made the same size as the one shown here, the blank (Fig. 43, at left) will need to be 1¾ in. thick. Other sizes may be taken

directly from the drawings, which are shown full size.

The dog shown here is whittled from aromatic red cedar. This wood carves well when a knife is used. A precaution which must be taken with cedar should be noted here, however. If the wood is checked or split in the slightest degree, it should be cast aside, since checking on this wood may go much deeper than appears on the surface, and it will get worse as the wood dries out after it has been carved. It is wiser to select a sound piece of wood before you begin to carve, rather than after a lot of work has been done on it.

After the blank has been cut on the band saw, a lot of the waste wood, such as that between the ears and the front legs, and that on both sides of the tail, may be sawed with a coping saw.

Step-by-step directions for carving the hound need not be given, since we believe the pictures pretty well indi-

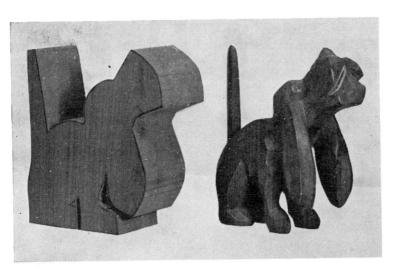

Fig. 43. The long-eared hound.

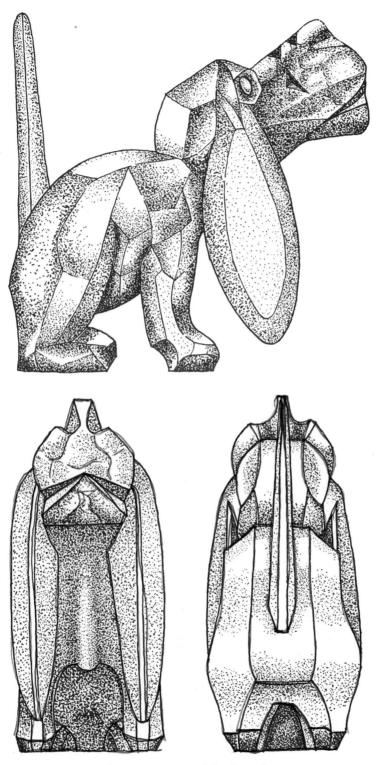

Fig. 44. Views of the hound.

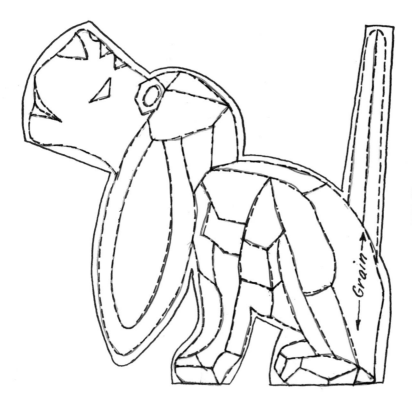

Fig. 45. Full-size pattern for the hound.

cate the steps to be followed. Carve the body first, then the legs and ears. Finish with the head. The final trimming should be done with long sweeping cuts of the knife wherever this is possible.

When the figure has been completed, apply wax and polish it with a soft cloth to a high gloss.

Alerted Fawn

If you like carving animals, the alerted fawn (Fig. 46) is an interesting one to try. A piece of California sugar pine (1⅝ in. thick, 2¾ in. wide, and 5½ in. long; straight-grained, and the grain running vertically) should be used. The pose is a bit unusual, but it is also different enough to be interesting. Trace the outline of Figure 47 to make a pattern for the blank. Additional sawing may be done to separate the legs.

The body of the fawn should give the whittler little trouble. It is very plain and simple. The legs are difficult only to the extent that being thin, care must be taken not to split off parts of the feet when carving them.

Some special care is needed when carving the eyes. See the photograph. They should bulge in their sockets. When carved, the pupils are painted black, and so also are the hooves.

A light grayish-brown color is used to stain the fawn, after which it is waxed and polished.

Fig. 46. The alerted fawn.

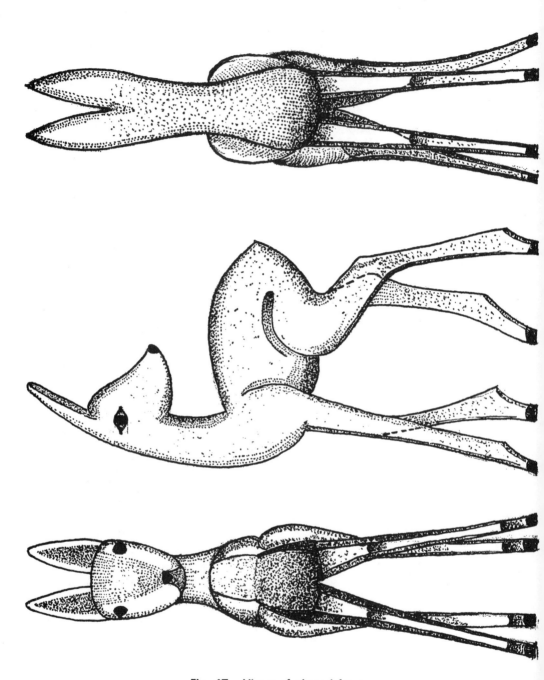

Fig. 47. Views of alerted fawn.

Feeding Fawn

The feeding fawn (Fig. 48) is somewhat more difficult to carve than the alerted fawn, and will take more time to carve. However, with so many views showing every side of it, one should not have too much trouble carving it. A piece of wood 2½ in. thick, 3⅞ in. wide, and 3⅝ in. long will be needed to carve it.

Use a pattern (Fig. 50) to saw it to shape, as shown on the side views. The blank may be sawed out on a band saw or a jig saw. Then make a pattern and saw it to shape as viewed from front or rear.

The feeding fawn will require careful work where the front leg and neck come close together.

Fig. 48. The feeding fawn.

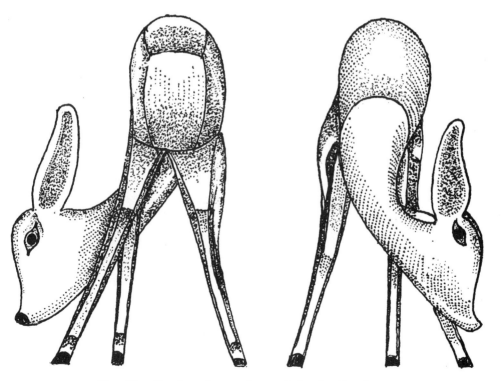

Fig. 49. Front and rear views of the feeding fawn.

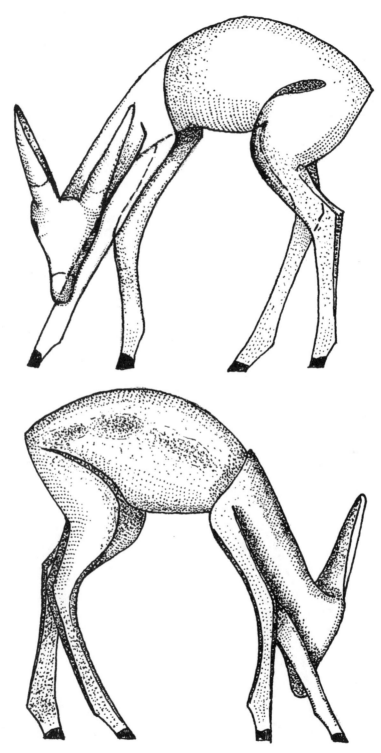

Fig. 50. Side views of feeding fawn.

Indian-Head Mask

The Indian-head mask (Fig. 51) gives good practice in carving a face, and makes a very nice wall decoration as well. The head may be made any desired size. The one shown here is 4 in. high (less the feather) (Fig. 52). Aromatic red cedar or mahogany are good woods to use to carve it. The one shown was carved of California red cedar, a very soft wood, but a wood whose grain markings add to the interest of the piece.

Saw the block of wood first to the shape shown in the profile view (Fig. 52). The grain should run vertically. Then saw it to the shape of the front view, after which it will be ready to

Fig. 51. The Indian-head mask.

Fig. 52. Pattern for the Indian-head mask.

carve. First cut the line separating the hair from the face. Round the part representing the hair and roughly shape it before cutting the deep grooves which make it look like hair.

Next round his forehead, shape his nose, and his cheeks with their high cheekbones so characteristic of the red man. The pupils of the eyes are pear-shaped slits cut into deep-set flat eye sockets. Carve the mouth, nostril holes, "crow's feet" on both eyes, and put in the lines on the forehead. A feather on top of his head completes the job and makes a real Indian out of him. The hair is painted black. When the paint has dried, polish the entire carving with wax.

Fig. 53. Views of the Indian-head mask.

Madonna Shrine

One of the outstanding carvings in this collection is the Madonna shrine (Fig. 54). Note the simplicity of the composition, the beauty and delicate detail of the face (Fig. 55).

Begin by cutting the blank on the band saw to the profile (Fig. 56). Then saw it to the shape of the front view. Next draw the outline of the face and hands. With a V tool, cut deep parting lines around these, and start forming the cheeks, chin, and forehead. Remove waste surrounding the hands, then round the hands to their approximate shape, leaving the shaping of the fingers until later. Draw the nose, eyes, mouth, and outline of the hair. These may then be carved.

When carving a face, no one of the above features is entirely completed without some work being done on the others. Individual features, however, such as the nose, will be given special attention both at the start of carving, and again at the end when the final touches are put on. As a general rule, the highest parts are started first. Thus, begin with the nose, and proceed from there to the next lowest levels like the chin, mouth, and forehead. The hair is little if any higher than the forehead, but the rounding over of the forehead permits the dividing line between it and the hair to be made. Carve the cheeks, grooving in around the edges with a fairly deep V line. Carve a hollow groove all around the lips and trim carefully. Complete the face by doing the eyes and eyebrows. Carve the hood or mantle.

Fig. 54. The Madonna shrine.

To carve the lower part, first round over the shelflike upper part of the bracket. Draw in the leaf and outline it with a V tool. Then lower the background surrounding the leaf slightly, after which the lower parts of the bracket, including the ball, which is spiraled, and the section above it on which the leaf appears, may be rounded over, as shown in the photograph and drawing.

Next, carefully draw the spirals on the ball, the reeding on the bracket, and the leaf details; then carve these parts.

Mahogany was used to carve the Madonna shown here. It was finished with wax and polished.

Fig. 55. Views of Madonna shrine.

Fig. 56. Patterns for the Madonna shrine.

Man From the Mennonite Country

The Pennsylvania Dutch country, in the heart of which are found the counties of Bucks, Berks, Lancaster, and Lehigh, contains some of the richest, most fertile farmland in the eastern United States. Many of these fine farms with their big red barns have been owned and operated for generations by the Amish and the Mennonites — many of whom still go about dressed in the quaint costumes shown being worn by our man and woman from the Mennonite country. Not all sects of Mennonites, however, wear this distinctive clothing.

California sugar pine is good wood to carve the man from the Mennonite country (Fig. 57). A block of wood measuring 1⅞ by 2¼ by 5½ in. will be needed to reproduce a carving as large as the original figure. First, make stiff paper patterns of the front and side (Fig. 59). Lay out the profile for the side view, shown at B, first. Saw this to shape on the band saw or jig saw. Then carefully trace the outline of the front, shown at A, and saw it to this shape. Holes may be drilled and then the waste sawed out to clear the area between his legs.

Next, draw important details such as the lines separating his arms from his body, the neck line, lines forming the lapel of his coat, the top of his trousers, and other main features. Do not bother at first to draw in fine details, such as eyes, mouth, or the lines which outline each knife cut. These will not be needed until the figure has assumed the approximate semblance of its final shape.

Fig. 57. Mennonite man.

To carve him, first score deep knife lines along the insides of his arms, and where his legs are joined to his body. Then begin trimming away the wood on both sides of these knife cuts, roughly rounding these parts of his body as you do so. At the same time start rounding his legs, forming his shoes, and the base upon which he stands.

Next, start rounding and shaping his hat and his face. When beginning work on his face, be particularly careful not to cut away too much wood on protruding elements, such as his nose, outcropping hair, and beard. Trim these to shape with extreme caution, drawing and re-drawing lines to outline various features since they are needed as guides to do the cutting.

52

In giving directions on how to do wood carving, it is not always possible, nor is it always desirable to give specific directions as to what cuts you shall make first, or what other cuts are to be made next. Some specific directions are needed to start the work, but pretty soon the actual sequence of future cuts must be planned as well as executed by the wood-carver himself. This will be easier if one has before him an actual model of the carving. However, by carefully checking the drawings (Figs. 58 and 59), and bolstered by the experience of having made several less difficult carvings previously, you will not have great difficulty in carving this figure.

On this carving the eyes are perhaps the most difficult detail, mostly because they are so small. The nose, mouth, and cheeks, being larger are more easily formed. The eyes, however, are slightly less than ⅛ in. wide vertically, and only about 3/16 in. wide horizontally. They bulge out slightly from deep sockets formed by the jutting brow above, and the bulging cheeks below them. A very fine black ink line, arched to outline the top of the eyeball gives just the right effect over the tiny round dot forming the pupil. The eyebrows also are thin black arched lines.

Water colors may be used to paint his coat, trousers, and hat black. His beard is a brick reddish-brown, and his face and shirt are white. His bulging cheeks and the tip of his nose are tinted a healthy cherry red, and his lips a deeper hue of the same. When the water colors used for this purpose have dried, polish him down with a coat of wax.

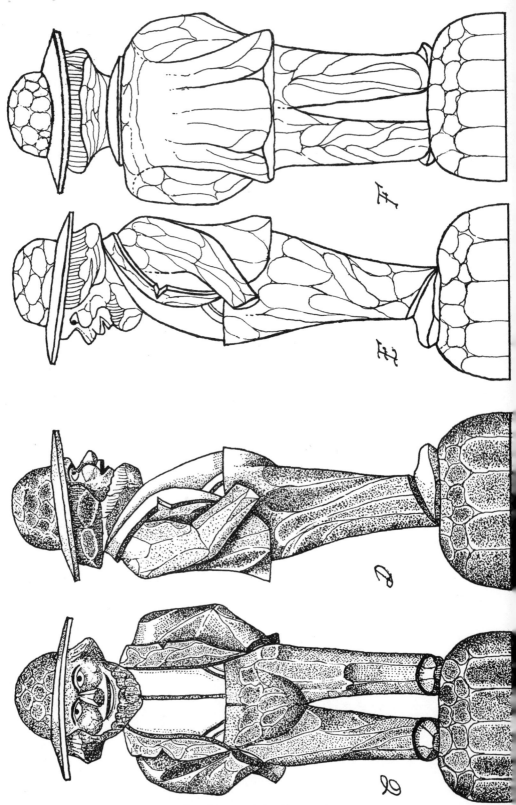

Fig. 58. Views of the Mennonite man.

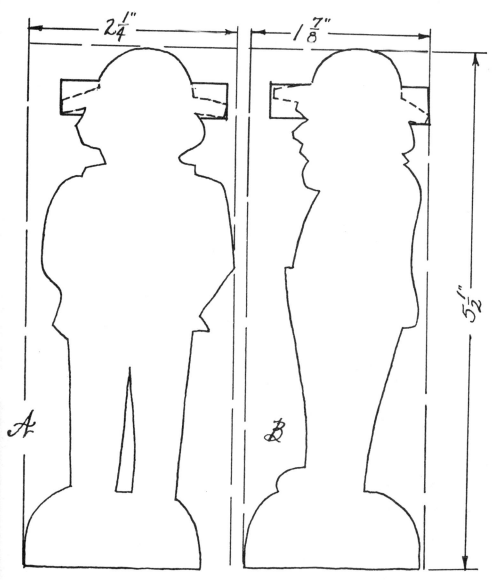

Fig. 59. Patterns for the Mennonite man.

Woman From the Mennonite Country

The woman from the Mennonite country (Fig. 60) is not quite as difficult to carve as the man because her dress is simpler than the clothes on the man. For this reason, possibly, she might even be attempted before the man, if both are to be carved.

First trace the pattern and cut the side shape, and then carefully draw the outline for the front view (Fig. 61). Draw the most important outlines, such as her waistline, bonnet strings, lines around her bonnet and the one outlining the bottom of her bonnet. Also draw the lines separating her arms from her body. Draw her shopping bag, the package she is carrying, and the hand holding the package. Also outline the face under the brim of the bonnet. When these lines have been drawn you are ready to start carving (Figs. 62 and 63).

First, strive for approximate shapes on all parts of the figure, leaving definite details until later. With the point of a sharp knife make deep incisions to outline the bonnet straps and the package in her right hand, these being raised above other elements on the upper part of her body. Trim around these to a depth of $\frac{1}{16}$ in. or more on each side of the bonnet straps, and a quarter of an inch or more around the package and the hand. Her bodice outline is also incised with the point of a sharp knife blade, and the parts around the regions of the upper arms are lowered a good $\frac{1}{16}$ in. or more, both in front and in back, as shown in the drawing and photograph.

Her dress and her bonnet are fairly simple to carve. There is some undercutting all around the shopping bag, and, of course, the hands should be very carefully formed. Make light incisions to separate each finger, then round them carefully, but not too deeply.

Once her body from the neck down, and the outside of the bonnet have been pretty well completed, start carving her face. Outline her face. The deepest cutting under the bonnet brim at the sides of her neck is $\frac{1}{2}$ in. Her chin protrudes from the neck $\frac{1}{4}$ in. The top of her head is $\frac{3}{16}$ in. back from the front of the bonnet brim. Her nose sticks out a full eighth of an inch from her upper lip. The eyes are set in rather deeply — $\frac{1}{8}$ in. from the highest point of the cheeks and forehead. The

Fig. 60. The Mennonite woman.

eyeballs are well rounded and are about the same size as they are on the Mennonite man.

When the figure is completed, paint her dress black. Her face and her bonnet underneath are white, as is the package in her right hand. Her lips are a cherry red, and the high parts of her cheeks are tinged with this color also. The eyeballs are outlined with very fine black lines. When the water colors used for this purpose have dried, wax and polish the project.

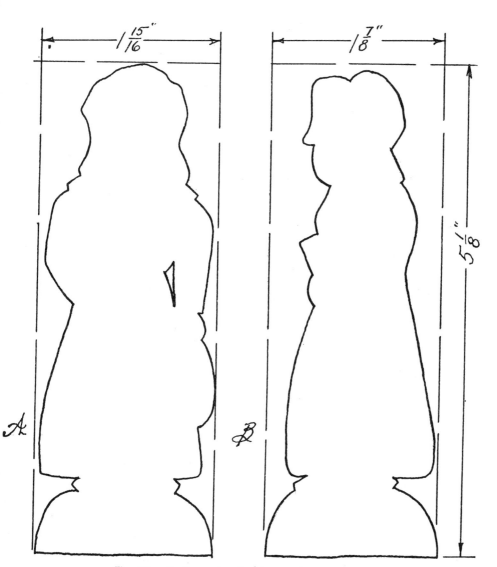

Fig. 61. Patterns for the Mennonite woman.

Fig. 62. Views of the Mennonite woman.

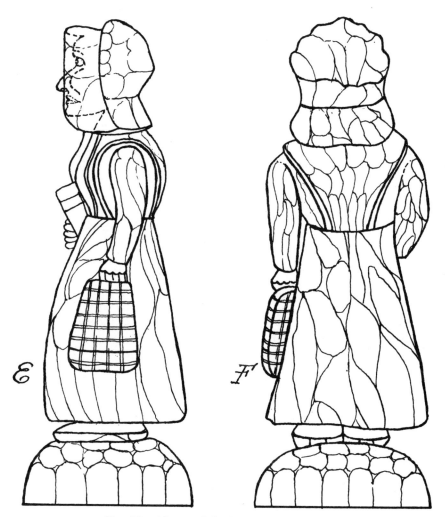

Fig. 63. Views of the Mennonite woman.

Question Mark

One of the delightful things about "Contemporary Design" is the fact that anyone's guess as to what the things are supposed to represent are as authoritative as the next person's. When one designs a dog, it must resemble a dog, or at least it must resemble a dog sufficiently so as not to be confused with some other familiar animal — a horse, for example. But when one designs in the contemporary vein, all the bars are down.

As to our little "Question Mark" (Fig. 64), you may name it anything you like, for what you name it will probably be as appropriate as what I have named it.

Once the blank has been cut out on the band saw, lay out as carefully as possible the positions and thicknesses of the head, neck, legs, tail, and other members which remain to be cut to size before being shaped. The rest consists of nothing much more than a rounding over of every part (Fig. 65), with the exception of the head which requires a little more modeling. Be sure when you saw him out, to place the pattern on the block of wood so the grain goes as indicated by the direction of the arrows (Fig. 65), in order to avoid splitting the wood on the legs, or the neck. The block of wood should be about 1½ in. thick.

On animals such as this, the author

Fig. 64. The Question Mark.

finds it best to do most of the carving and shaping before cutting out the waste wood which separates the legs; leaving this until nearly last so there is less danger of breaking the legs. Also the waste wood provides a good area for clamping or holding the figure in a vise.

Once the figure has been carved, it is carefully sanded until absolutely smooth. A good way to do this is to cut fairly long narrow strips of fine garnet paper, and while the carving is held in the vise, pull the garnet strip back and forth over the carving while holding the garnet strip by both ends. Final sanding should be done with the grain only, using 6/0 garnet paper. Finish the figure with floor wax and polish it to a high luster.

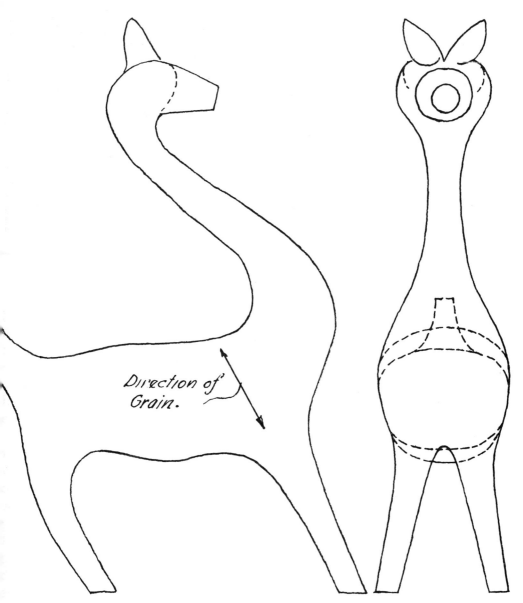

Direction of Grain.

Fig. 65. Patterns for Question Mark.

Bird

The bird shown in Figure 67 is a very simple carving and yet, one which can be given considerable interest by using colors to decorate it in various ways. They may be used with flower arrangements (as may many of the other carvings in this book), placed on a shelf or mantel, or used decoratively in countless other ways.

The drawing shows three views of the bird, to help the wood-carver get the correct shape (Fig. 69). Once the pattern (Fig. 68) has been drawn on white pine, and sawed out on a band saw, the carving will consist of little more than rounding over corners, since

Fig. 67. The bird.

there is a minimum of shaping on this project. This makes it a very fine carving for a beginner to try.

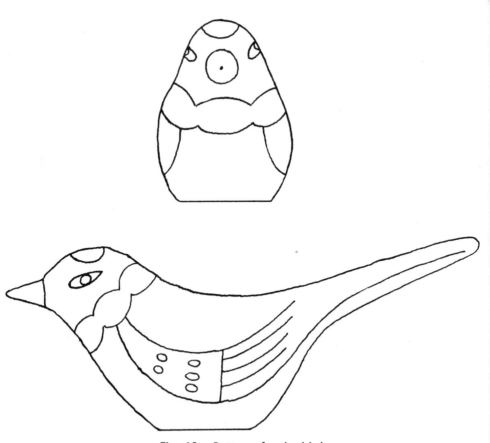

Fig. 68. Patterns for the bird.

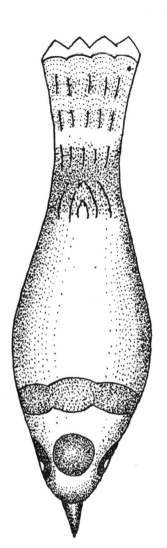
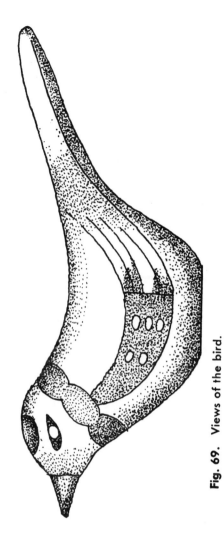

Fig. 69. Views of the bird.

Spoon Rack and Mirror With Drawer

One may obtain some very interesting effects with line carving, as may be seen by looking at Figures 72–78. Line carving is a valuable means of learning tool techniques, such as control of the chisel as it is being forced through the wood by employing the various methods we have mentioned (p. 23). It also helps to familiarize one with the grain structures of various types of wood, and how they respond to the chisel as it is pushed or driven in various directions. One soon learns when it is better to carve with a series of short strokes, rather than with fewer long sweeps of the tool, or vice versa. The proper angle at which the tool should be held to make various kinds of cuts, or to get a variety of effects, is another thing which may be learned by doing simple types of carving such as this. Learning them on simple jobs like these is much easier than on a job which requires considerable modeling.

The spoon rack (Fig. 72) and the mirror with drawer (Figs. 73 and 74) are two examples of what may be done with this kind of carving on objects of considerable practical value. The spoon rack is decoratively embellished with ornament consisting for the most part of simple line carving like the Pennsylvania Dutch heart and leaf motifs; and simple chip carving like the diamond, the rosette at the bottom, and the star medallion in the center; and

simple gouge work, like the rosette at the top. The backgrounds are further embellished with stamping tools to give contrast to the background. Here a little bit of very elementary tool work adds a wealth of character to a simple object.

The bird-and-heart motif on the lower part of the mirror with drawer consists of the same elementary type of line carving, but it goes a step farther in the embellishment of the wooden surface, in that the design is colored with either paint or stain. The part shown in black on the drawing may be painted or stained black, or other colors may be used. The part shown with the dotted background may be painted still another color, or it may first be decorated with stamping tools, and then colored. Transparent colors are recommended over stamped backgrounds.

The heart motif in the medallion at the top of the mirror requires some modeling, and the background of this medallion has been removed on the jig saw. The scrolls, which are quite simple to carve, also enhance the decorative effect of this top member.

The bands forming the hearts of this upper member are done with a gouge. The buds inside the hearts are convex, and are shaped by rounding their edges with a skew chisel. The leaflike portion of the bud is raised about $\frac{1}{16}$ in. or slightly more above the bud itself, and carefully rounded over on the outside.

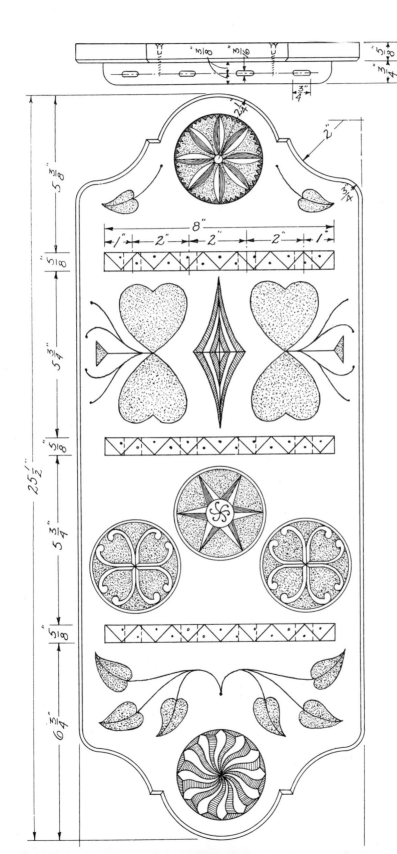

Fig. 72. The spoon rack.

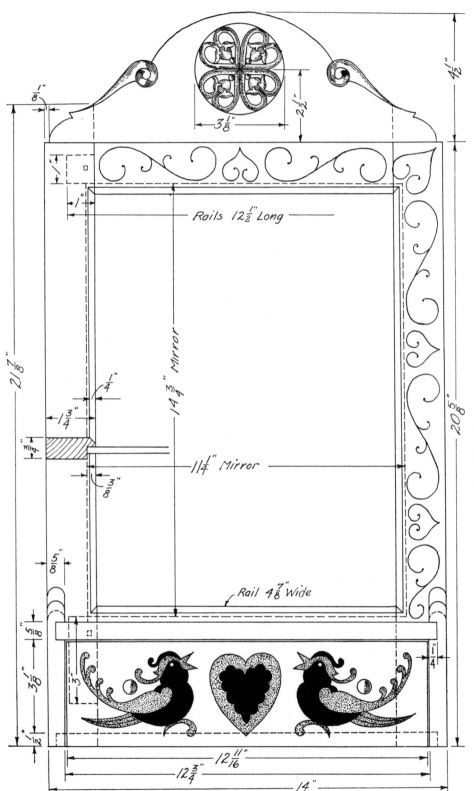

Fig. 73. Mirror with drawer.

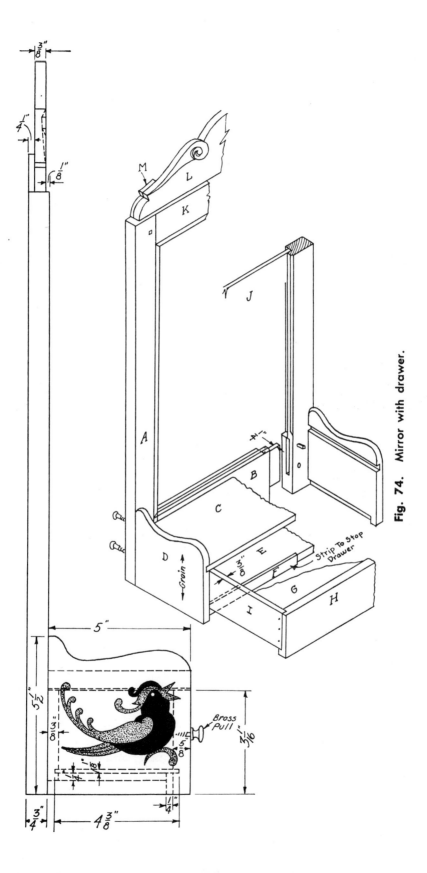

Fig. 74. Mirror with drawer.

Table Mats

These mats are easy to carve (Figs. 76, 77, and 78). The boards may be used like a tile or mat, on the dining table, to place under a dish of hot food. Each consists of a piece of hard maple, or birch, ½ in. thick by 6 in. square, on which the design is carved with a very shallow gouge. A hard wood, such as maple, is recommended for carving this, because maple is a close-grained wood and of sufficient hardness to cut cleanly, provided sharp carving chisels are used; for contrary to general belief among those who have never tried to carve, softwoods are more difficult to carve than hardwoods. Greater skill and sharper tools are needed to carve softwoods, since the wood fibers have a tendency to yield rather than be severed under anything except the keenest edges.

First, lay out the design with a pencil. The design may be traced full-size on tracing paper, and transferred directly from this to the wood. Usually, if a soft pencil is used to trace the design, it will leave clear outlines on the wood when carefully gone over with a harder pencil on the opposite side of the tracing paper. Carbon paper may be used to transfer a design, but it has a tendency to smudge badly, and this ofttimes obscures parts of the outline. Drawing the design directly on the wood with a pencil is best, provided one has the skill.

When the design has been transferred to the wood (Fig. 76), clamp the board to the top of a workbench. Holding the gouge at an angle of about 60 degrees, strike it a light, quick blow with the mallet, as shown in the sketch (Fig. 75). Each petal of

Fig. 75. Striking the gouge.

the simple rosette, and each link of the chainlike border requires at least two blows, one from either side, plus a little trimming to clean it up after the chip of wood has been removed.

Carving such as this requires no sanding if carefully done. It is important to try to cut cleanly, using sharp tools, when beginning to carve. The mark of the tool is not detrimental, but adds character to the carving. One must, however, learn to distinguish between slipshod haphazard cutting, and the crisp, clean, purposeful cutting that results from practice.

The inexperienced wood-carver has a tendency to make many unnecessary cuts, largely because he is not quite capable of visualizing his goal. Practice in actual carving, coupled with careful observation, should give him a better perception of form, thus improving the quality of his work.

Figures 77 and 78 are two more examples of simple line carving. This type of carving is done with either a very fine veining tool which cuts a very narrow U-shaped line, or with a V tool. See pages 22 and 23.

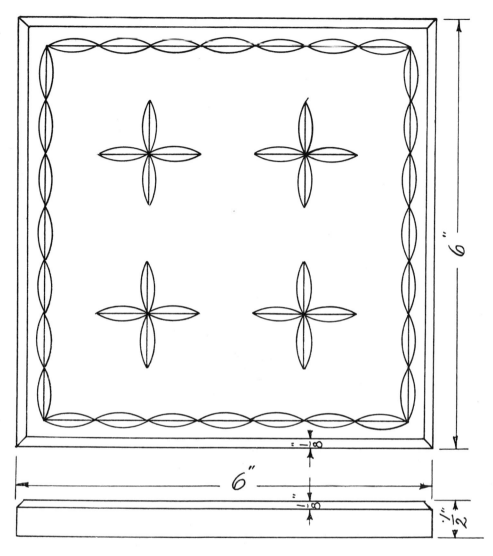

Fig. 76. A table mat.

Fig. 77. A table mat.

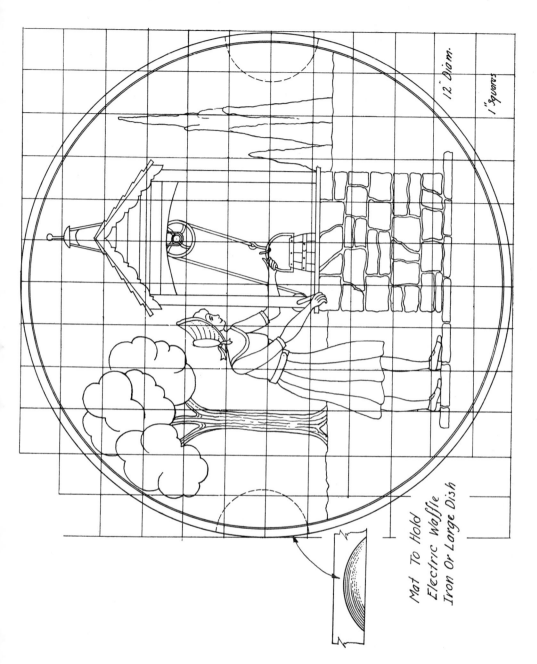

Fig. 78. A table mat.

Autumn Harvest

A very handsome plaque, and one which is quite suitable for the dining room, is autumn harvest (Fig. 79). Modeling this plaque, while not exceedingly difficult, must, nevertheless, be meticulously executed. Each grape must be outlined and then carefully rounded. The driftwood, and dried twigs, must be outlined and then modeled. On the driftwood the deeply shaded parts are cut low with a narrow U-shaped gouge, and twisting the gouge, first to one side then to the other as you push it along, will give the proper effect on these parts. The higher parts represented by lighter lines may be finished off with shallow sweeping cuts, closely paralleling each other and done with a fine veiner. The twigs, once they are properly modeled, may be finished off with a veiner in the same way, and so also may the corn husks.

Each grain of wheat should be carefully outlined, then just as carefully rounded over. The same is true of each kernel of corn, after the ear as a whole has first been properly modeled to give the illusion of its being round. We say the illusion of being round, because the amount of actual rounding of objects against a background cut no deeper than $\frac{1}{4}$ or $\frac{3}{8}$ in. is somewhat limited. Notice the wavy effect on the corn husk, achieved by ever so slightly hollowing the more deeply shaded areas across the husk with a shallow gouge before carving the even shallower grooves which run lengthwise.

When each part of the design has been carved, carefully smooth the background. Then go over every part of it with a No. 4 extra flat, to simulate the effect shown in Figure 79.

This plaque will look best if the wood color is left as nearly natural as possible. Use mahogany, walnut, butternut, or some other close-grained hardwood, having a grain on which there is as little figure as possible, and finish it with wax or with a well-rubbed hard oil finish. A pattern for this plaque is shown in Figure 80.

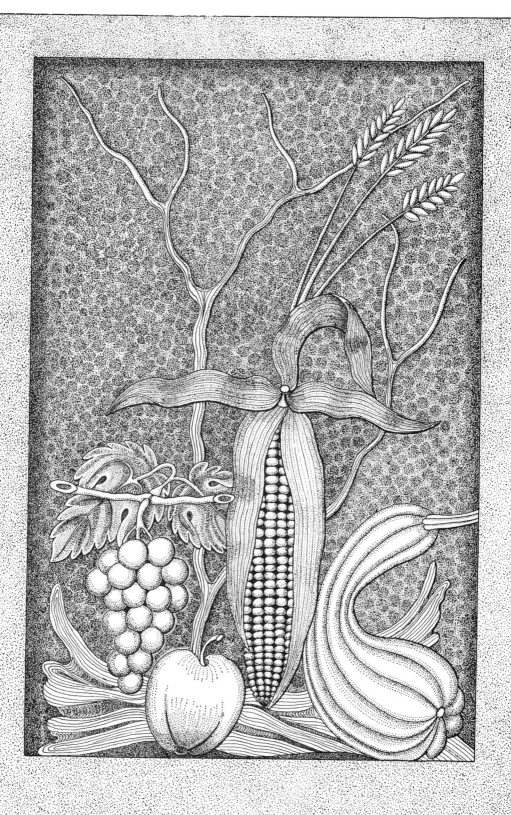

Fig. 79. Autumn harvest.

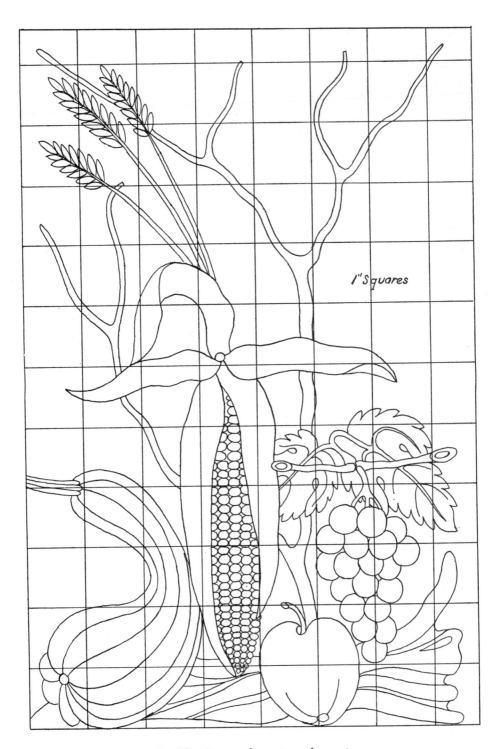

Fig. 80. Pattern for autumn harvest.

Eagle

The eagle is a truly regal looking bird. We have tried to capture and transmit to wood this characteristic of the bird. The plaque shown in Figure 81 was carved on walnut by Dr. Russell Borneman, who did a remarkably fine piece of work.

The background immediately surrounding the eagle is cut to a depth of ½ in. A slightly deeper groove outlines this background on three sides.

The modeling for the carving is not very difficult, and even a beginner should have little trouble doing it (Fig. 82). Giving the eagle the proper surface treatment to simulate the feathers on his wing, head, and other parts of his body is somewhat more difficult, and should be done with painstaking care. Special attention should be given to the down on his head and around the lower parts of his legs. This down should be carved with short cuts, using a wobbling motion to push the fine veiner through the wood. This gives the grooves a slightly roughened texture which simulates the down of feathers about as realistically as we know how, on wood.

The eagle's eye is set deep in its socket, which drops sharply above the eye, but slopes more gently toward it at the bottom and sides.

Boiled linseed oil was the only finish applied to this plaque. Repeated coats vigorously rubbed to a polish bring out the full beauty of the grain.

Fig. 81. The eagle.

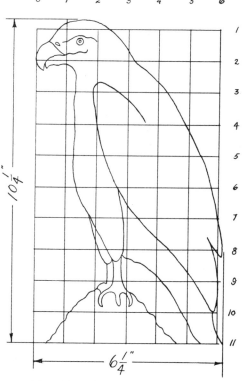

Fig. 82. Pattern for the eagle.

Fig. 83.   The eagle plaque.

Pop-Up Playing Card Holder

The neat little box with the dog-wood blossoms carved on top holds two packs of playing cards (Figs. 83 and 84). When the button is pressed down, two flaps inside the box swing upward on pivots, and the two packs of cards are raised up out of the box. A cutaway drawing, showing how the button operates the flaps, and construction details for making the box are shown in Figure 85.

The box itself is constructed of ¼-in. plywood. White pine plywood was used in this case, but birch veneered plywood would do as well. Fir plywood should not be used, since it would not result in as nice a job. Careful fitting and pivoting of the lids and flaps is necessary to insure good operation when the flaps are being raised. The lids may be made of yellow poplar, maple, or birch, since they are to be carved and must therefore be made of solid stock instead of plywood.

The dogwood blossom was painted

Fig. 84. Pop-up playing card holder.

an off-white, with a touch of brown at the end of each petal. The leaves and stem are green, and the background is painted in gold. The entire surface was then given several coats of varnish and rubbed down with pumice stone and oil.

A full-sized pattern for laying out the carving on the lids is shown in Figure 86.

As we proceed in our work in wood carving, it becomes evident that as the work becomes more difficult it also becomes more interesting. This is so because the more advanced types of wood carving open up to us the opportunity for greater variety of design.

Fig. 85. View of the card holder.

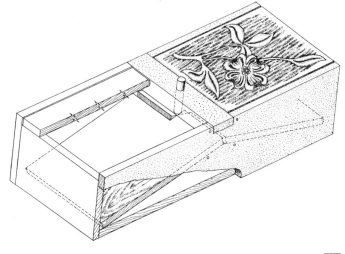

77

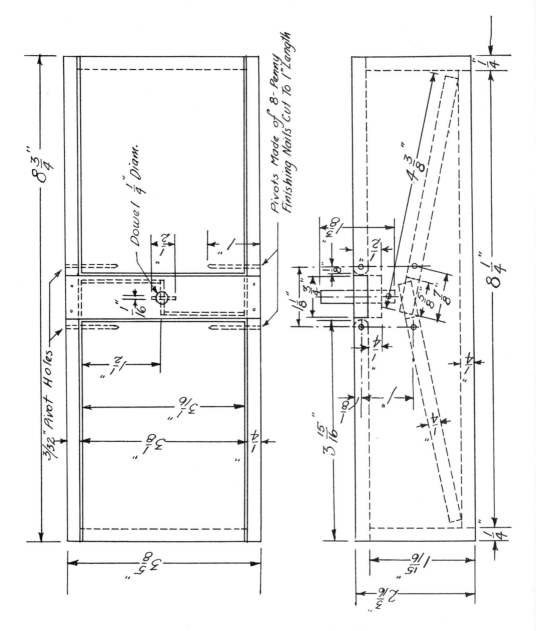

Fig. 86. Construction details of card holder.

Fig. 87. Full-size pattern for box decoration.

Fireplace Bellows

Another useful project decorated with flat-surface carving is the fireplace bellows shown in Figure 89. The author made these bellows many years ago and they are still giving very fine service. Mahogany, walnut, birch, or maple are good materials to use in making the bellows.

Fig. 89. The fireplace bellows.

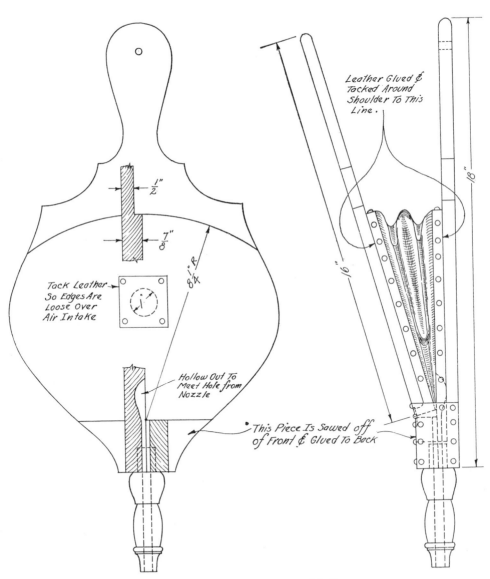

Leather Glued & Tacked Around Shoulder To This Line.

Tack Leather So Edges Are Loose Over Air Intake

$\frac{1}{2}$"

$\frac{7}{8}$"

8½" R

Hollow Out To Meet Hole from Nozzle

This Piece Is Sawed off of Front & Glued To Back

18"

16"

Fig. 90. Construction details of bellows.

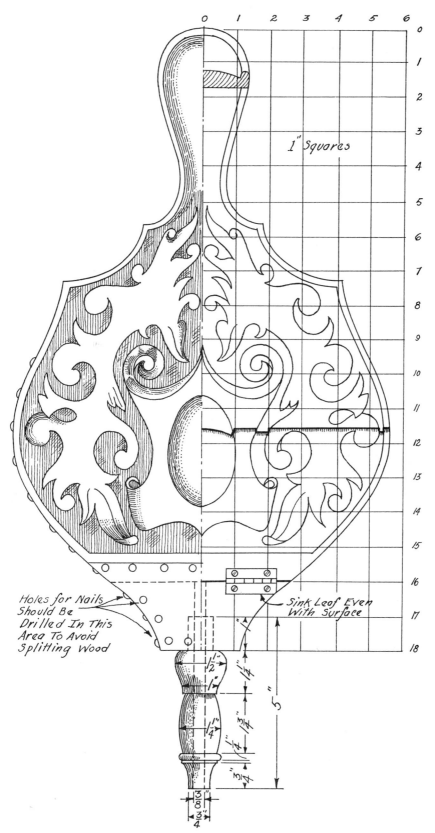

Fig. 91. Design for fireplace bellows.

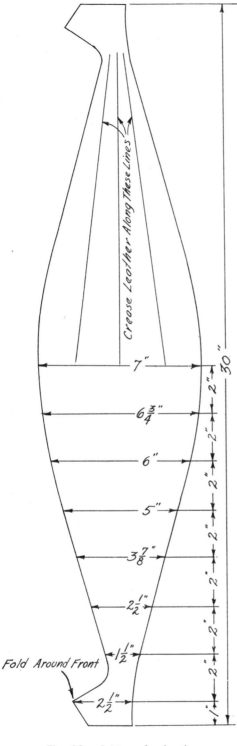

Crease Leather Along These Lines

7"

6¾"

6"

5"

3⅞"

2½"

1½"

Fold Around Front

2½"

2"
2"
2"
2"
2"
2"
2"

30"

Fig. 92. Pattern for leather.

To build the bellows, two pieces of stock measuring ⅞ by 11 by 18 in. are required, and one piece 1¾ in. square by about 8 in. long for the nozzle. A piece of kid leather 7 by 30 in. is also required. About 75 upholstering nails are needed to fasten the leather to the sides. Notice that on this project there is a little bit of modeling on the scrolls, the lower leaves, and the cobochen. This modeling adds additional interest to the design.

First, draw a full-sized pattern like the one shown on the right half of Figure 91. Transfer this to the wood and saw the pieces to shape on the band saw. Cut the shoulders on the inside of the front and back members, as shown in Figure 90. Most of this work may be done with a router bit on the drill press, if such equipment is available. This will leave the handles only ½ in. thick, and the part below them ⅞ in. thick with room to tack on the leather (Fig. 90).

Round the edges of the handles, and then cut off the bottom 2 in. of the front, and glue it to the inside of the back, as shown in Figure 90. Bore the vent hole and tack a small piece of leather over it to form the air valve. Turn and drill the nozzle, then bore a hole through the bottom end of the bellows and glue the nozzle to the bellows.

Next, start the carving by incising the lines of the design with a veiner, or by cutting the outlines with chisels. Lower the background to a depth of about ⅛ in. with gouges. Trim all outlines and edges carefully. Tool marks on the background will, and should, show, but they should be so carefully leveled out that the finished background will show interesting texture. Carelessness in smoothing the background will denote shoddy workmanship.

When the carving is completed, fasten the front to the back with hinges as shown in Figure 91. Sink the hinges so they are level with the surface.

Kid leather may be bought in a variety of colors. Cut the leather to the shape shown in Figure 92, and crease it along the lines indicated, after first wetting the leather. This will make it fold properly when the bellows are compressed.

When the leather's dry, start gluing and tacking it to the wood by first marking the centers of both the leather and the shoulders to which it will be glued. Use a tube of household cement to glue the leather to the shoulders, and around the edges of the front and back. Glue only a small area at a time,

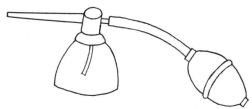

Fig. 93.   A powder blower.

and nail it down as you go. Bring the ends down and lap them over the hinges. Glue, but do not nail these ends until a second piece of leather has been fitted around the lower end; then nail them as shown in Figure 91. Drill nail holes a little smaller in diameter than the nails where this is indicated on Figures 90 and 91.

The raised part of the pattern may be stained a darker color than the background. The background is painted gold, then tinted with violet, crimson, and green bronze powders around the edges of the raised parts. The bronze powders may be blown on over a tacky varnished surface with a powder blower (Fig. 93).

The Expanding Bookstall

The expanding bookstall is a project which lends itself well to the use of level surface carving. Figure 94 shows a rather simple design which may be used to decorate the bookstall.

The bookstall should first be made and assembled before carving is started (Fig. 95). The sticks going crosswise below the bed may be removed to carve the ends, and replaced when the carving has been completed. The expanding bed may be made of sticks of wood of any desired length, depending upon how many books you want the project to hold. Mahogany, oak, maple, walnut, or birch are excellent for carving, and would all be suitable for this particular job. The ends of the sticks are mortised through the bookends, glued in place, and may then be carved as easily as the other parts of the surface.

First, draw or transfer the design upon the surface to be carved. Then with a V tool, or a fine veiner, outline the entire design to a depth of not more than $\frac{1}{16}$ in. This should be done on every one of the lines, even where the vertical fingerlike scrolls join the other scrolls at the bottom of Figure 94. Once the background of the design has been cut down with a flat gouge, a meeting place, such as is shown near the bottom of Figure 94 is usually lowered to the depth of this background where the two parts meet. This makes it appear as though this lowered part lies below, or springs from beneath the higher surface adjoining it. This lowering should be done so gradually that it slopes from about the middle of the vertical finger-like scrolls, reaching its greatest depth where they are joined to the curved scrolls below them. This sloping is indicated by the slightly deeper shading on this part of the surface (Fig. 94). Once this effect has been achieved, the background immediately surrounding this area may be cut still a little deeper. Indeed, all of the remaining background may also be cut a little deeper than it was at first, though some judgment about limiting its depth will have to be used to make it conform to the scale and size of the design. Generally speaking, it should not be very deep, not more than $\frac{1}{8}$ in. at the most in this case.

It is important to keep the outline of the design clean and sharp. Very often, in order to achieve this, it will be necessary to finish up around all the edges by driving the chisel straight down into the wood with a mallet, as shown in Figure 28. As a matter of fact, many wood-carvers prefer to do their outlining in this manner right from the start, claiming this gives a sharper and more accurate outline. The author has always preferred to outline the design first with a V tool, staying a little outside the line, and then trim to the line later, because in that way there is less chance of driving the tool too deeply into the wood. In any case it is essential to achieve a clean, clear-cut outline when the job is finished.

Several methods of finishing the lowered background may be used. Probably the best is to trim it down all over to as level a surface as possible by using gouges with very shallow curvature — No. 3 or No. 4 sweep — (Fig. 96). To anyone who has done little or no carving this may seem quite

Fig. 94. Design for the expanding bookstall.

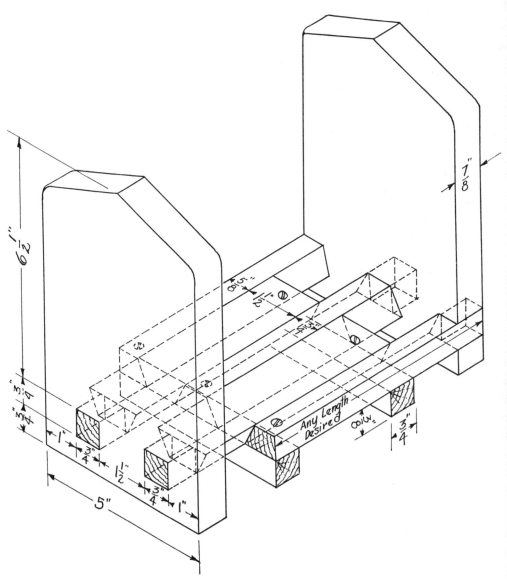

Fig. 95. Construction details for the expanding bookstall.

simple, but until it has actually been tried one does not realize the care necessary to achieve a satisfactory background. Where surfaces are fairly large and accessible to the tool, little difficulty will be encountered. The really hard part is to get equally clean and smooth surfaces in the tight corners. Such a background will look best

if all the tool cuts are made to go as nearly as possible in the same direction. With patience and care all this is possible. Other interesting backgrounds are achieved in various ways. A somewhat different one may be gotten by using stamping tools to mark the background. Such tools are shown in Figure 4. Still another method of

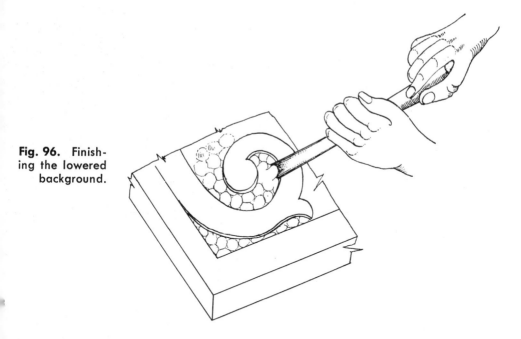

Fig. 96. Finishing the lowered background.

treating a background is to paint it some color which contrasts with the color on the surface. This could be gold bronzing powder blown on with a powder blower (Fig. 93) over wet varnish. Water colors may be used for a transparent effect and do not hide the grain of the wood, but accentuate it, especially after waxing and polishing. The background may even be gold-leafed if one knows how to do the work.

Gothic Box

In the Gothic box (Fig. 97), the leaves of the design include modeling of the surface instead of outlining, lowering the background, and leaving the surface flat as were the elements in the level-surface designs. The modeling is more or less crudely done, in keeping with much of the carving in the Gothic tradition. The shaping is, however, sufficiently well designed to give a good indication of what it is supposed to represent. The leaves and background areas were painted after being carved. The background inside the circle was painted crimson and stippled with gold. Painter's tinting colors — green, yellow, and orange — were carefully blended into the design by brushing them on and rubbing them with the tips of the fingers.

The construction of the box is shown in Figure 98. Trace the design from Figure 99, and transfer it to the wood to carve. The tracery on the front and ends of the box may easily be worked out with a compass and a ruler.

The Gothic tracery is carved in three levels. Since the leaves which comprise the other parts of the design are almost level with the surface, they must be outlined and shaped with the carving chisels at the same time the tracery is being done. In outlining these parts, or any parts of a carving for that matter, be sure to clamp the work firmly to the top of the workbench. Do not let it lie loose, for if you do the chisels will not easily sink into the wood but will tend to bounce when you strike the handle of the tool. In shaping the leaves, the darker the shading the deeper the cutting.

Fig. 97. The Gothic box.

The white or highlighted parts are level, or nearly level, with the surface of the box top. The parts with the darkest shading are at least ⅛ in. deep or a little deeper. An exception to this is the background inside the circle which, though lightly shaded, is as deep as the deepest part of the remainder of the background area.

Shaping the beads on the long leaves may constitute a problem to anyone who has never tried carving beads before. To do them, first cut a deep V-shaped trough on both sides of the row. Then make the beads square by making V cuts across from one of these V-shaped troughs to the other. This should be done with a narrow straight chisel held at a steep angle, and tapped very lightly with a mallet. Or it may be pushed into the wood by the pressure of the hand from two directions, after first having made a vertical incision with the chisel. Care must be taken at this point not to break off any of the beads by driving the chisel into the wood too hard. Now trim off the corners of each bead to make them octagon shaped, still using a narrow straight chisel with a very keen edge. Little, if any, further shaping need be done on the beads

Fig. 98.   The carved box.

Fig. 99. Full-size patterns for carving.

of this design, but if you want them completely round, trim them very carefully with a sharply curved narrow gouge, using the inside curve of the gouge against the bead.

The hinges on the box are hand-hammered copper, 18 gauge. If mak-ing the barrel of the hinge seems to difficult, a simpler method is to us small brass butts, fastening them i the conventional manner, and the butt the other parts of the hing against the barrel (Fig. 98).

Hand Carved Serving Tray

The hand carved serving tray (Figs. 100 and 101) is attractive and useful, and the modeling on the grapevine type of carving is rather easily done. The construction of the tray itself is similar to the construction of a picture frame. As a matter of fact, we are grouping trays and picture frames in this chapter because of elements of similarity in their construction or use.

The tray is made and assembled before it is carved (Fig. 102). About 35 or more inches of molding, shaped as shown in the cross-section view (Fig. 103), will be needed to make the frame. Rabbet one or more sticks of wood to hold the plywood bottom. Birch, walnut, or mahogany will be well suited to carve this tray, though the one shown was made of oak. Once the sticks have been rabbeted, the top of the molding may be shaped with a spokeshave or a plane. After sanding it smooth the sides and ends may be cut to length and the corners mitered for nailing together.

Drill nail holes into the mitered ends (Fig. 104). Fasten one piece of molding in the vise, put glue on the joint, and drive the brad which stands alone, first. Let the end of this side extend a bit when starting to nail, so that by the time the brad is driven into the wood the corners will be even. Fasten the piece, just nailed, in the vise and drive the two remaining brads. It is also a good idea to set the nailheads, so the holes may be closed with plastic wood. Continue in this manner to join all four corners, gluing and nailing each one in succession.

Make patterns and transfer the design to the wood (Fig. 106). The tray bottom may be fastened to the frame either before or after carving; but if it is fastened before the tray is carved, care will have to be taken to prevent chisel marks from marring its surface. A good plywood, surfaced with veneer made of the same wood as the frame, is recommended for use in the tray.

Figure 105 shows how to start carving the tray. This same method of starting to carve may be applied to

Fig. 100.
Serving tray.

Fig. 101. View of serving tray.

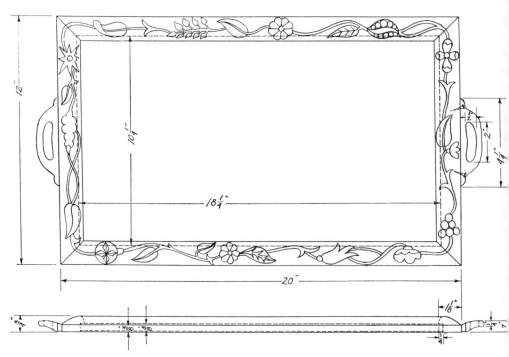

Fig. 102. Construction details of serving tray.

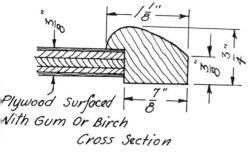

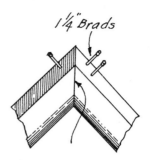

Plywood Surfaced
With Gum Or Birch
Cross Section

Fig. 103. Cross-section
view.

Fig. 104. Fastening
miter joints.

many subsequent jobs on which modeling is to be done. The design is first outlined with a V tool, as shown at A. On the type of carving used here, the V tool will do a faster job than if chisels of various shapes were driven directly down into the wood, as is often done on carvings on which the background is to be lowered before the design is modeled. In this design some of the background remains as high as the surface of the design. The design is brought into relief by trimming away only a little of the background directly adjacent to the design. This is done with extra flats, as shown at B, skew chisels, or even with a V tool. The leaves and flowers are then shaped and modeled (Fig. 101), using a skew as shown at C (Fig. 105), or carving chisels of other shapes, as

called for by the type of modeling being done.

When the carving has been done, and cleaned up with fine sandpaper, the handles should be made of hardwood, such as walnut or maple, and fastened to the tray. A piece of felt may be glued to the bottom of the tray if so desired.

The finish on the tray shown was a light-colored solution of burnt umber and turpentine. This was later given a coat of sealer. The sealer was rubbed down with steel wool, then the tray was waxed and polished. A very nice effect may be obtained if traces of gold are brushed on very sparingly all around the carved design before putting on the sealer. Tinting parts of the design with color can also achieve interesting results if it is not overdone.

Fig. 105. Using a skew.

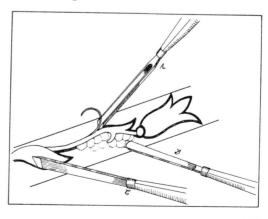

93

½ "Squares

Fig. 106.   Patterns to lay out the design.

Picture Frames

Making and carving picture frames Fig. 108) presents much the same roblems as making the serving tray ve have just described. The width of he molding should be determined to ome extent by the size of the picture) be framed. The scale of the orna- ent on the frame will also be affected y the size and type of picture to be ut into the frame. The designs (Figs.)7 and 109) do not pose any new roblems to those who have done at ast one of each type of carving thus r described.

Figure 107 has a level surface design ith a simple modern design and nice owing lines, while the other designs llow more along traditional lines. In l cases the size of the frame should first be determined, and the frame should be made before the design is drawn on it. In this way the design may best be properly adjusted to the frame. Two molding shapes are shown in Figure 110.

The frame shown in Figures 108 and 109 has a motif more difficult to carve than any of the others. It is a very interesting type of grapevine carving with a slightly Gothic flavor. The size may be varied to suit specific needs by the graph-square method described on page 31.

Once the design has been trans- ferred to the frame it should be out- lined very carefully with chisels of various shapes, as called for by the contour of the outline. The background need not be lowered very much —

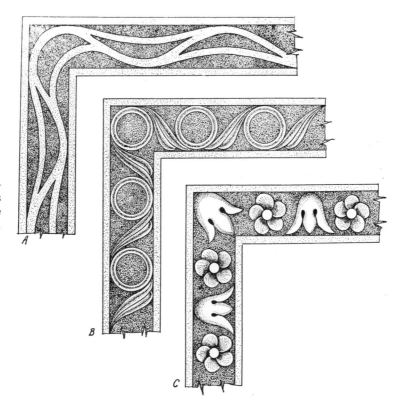

Fig. 107. Alternate patterns for picture frame.

Fig. 108. View of picture frame.

not more than ⅛ in. at most. The rounding of the grapes is done by first cutting straight down around each grape (not too deep at first) and then carefully trimming each one until they have all been rounded. Grapes in the middle of the bunch may be left higher than those on the outside. Stems of the grapevine are not lowered where they are joined to the top of a bunch, or the top of a leaf, but they are trimmed to a lower level where they appear to come from beneath a leaf or bunch of grapes. Deeper shading on a leaf (Fig. 108) denotes deeper cutting, while highlights denote areas almost level with the surface. A little practice should soon acquaint the amateur with the proper way of doing it.

Fig. 110. Molding shapes.

Fig. 109. Full-size pattern for design.

Snack Tray

Considerably different in construction and appearance from the other tray already described is the snack tray (Fig. 111). In this tray the dovetailed corners lend as much interest as the carved designs. Both, together with the rakish angle at which the sides and ends are joined, combine to make this a very interesting item.

Figures 112 and 113 show how to lay out and make the sides and ends of the tray. Mahogany, birch, walnut, yellow poplar, or even white pine may be used to make the tray. The sides should be made ⅜ in. thick. Note carefully that the ends of the sides, and of the endpieces must be slanted so they are ⅛ in. longer on the inside than they are on the outside. This must be done before the dovetailing is laid out.

Some craftsmen will prefer to make the pin members first, and hold them on the sides to mark the tail members, using a sharp scriber, or a sharp knife. Others prefer to reverse the order by cutting the tail members first. The dimensions for making the dovetail joints are given in Figures 112 and 113.

Grooves are cut for fastening the partitioning members, of which the piece into which the handle has been cut, is one (Figs. 114 and 115). Notice that these grooves are not cut clear across the ends and sides, but stop at the floor of the tray. The tray should be assembled, and all joints glued, and then thoroughly sanded. When this has been done it is ready to have the design drawn on the sides and ends for carving (Fig. 110).

Little need be said about how to do this carving except that the method of doing it should be the same as that employed in carving the serving tray. The cross-section views show the contour of the hearts and leaves which comprise the design.

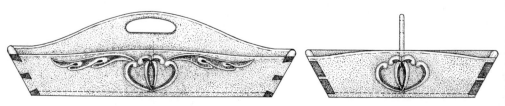

Fig. 111. The snack tray.

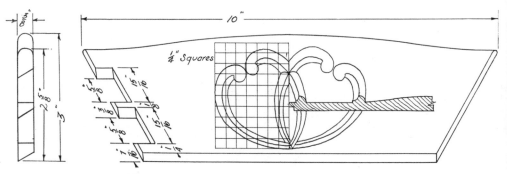

Fig. 112. Construction and design for ends.

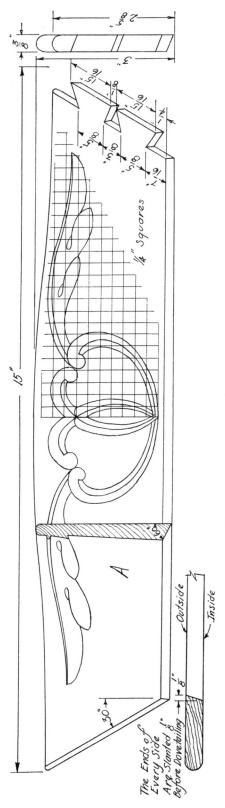

The Ends of
Every Side
Are Slanted ⅛"
Before Dovetailing

¼" squares

Fig. 113. Construction and design of sides.

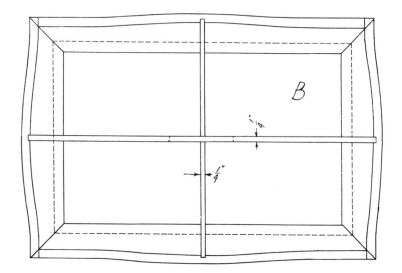

Fig. 114. Top view of snack tray.

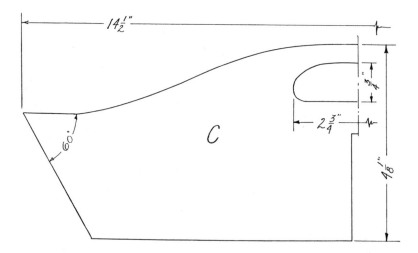

Fig. 115. Side view of snack tray handle.

Spice Cabinets

Quite often a very little bit of carving will do a great deal to enhance the beauty and value of an object upon which it appears. We think this is true of the spice cabinets (Fig. 119). A very simply carved sunburst at the top of the cabinet is the only decoration needed to set these aside as being a bit out of the ordinary.

Figure 120 shows the same design with an additional sunburst carved on the lower drawer. A double sunburst at the top — one in which the carving would come full circle, instead of forming only a semicircle — could also be used.

The spice cabinets will be useful and intriguing, hung in almost any room of the house. The two shown were built of white pine. The working drawing (Fig. 120) is sufficiently detailed to build either the single or the double cabinet. Patterns for the carving and scroll-sawed parts are found at the right of Figure 120.

Fig. 119.
Spice cabinets.

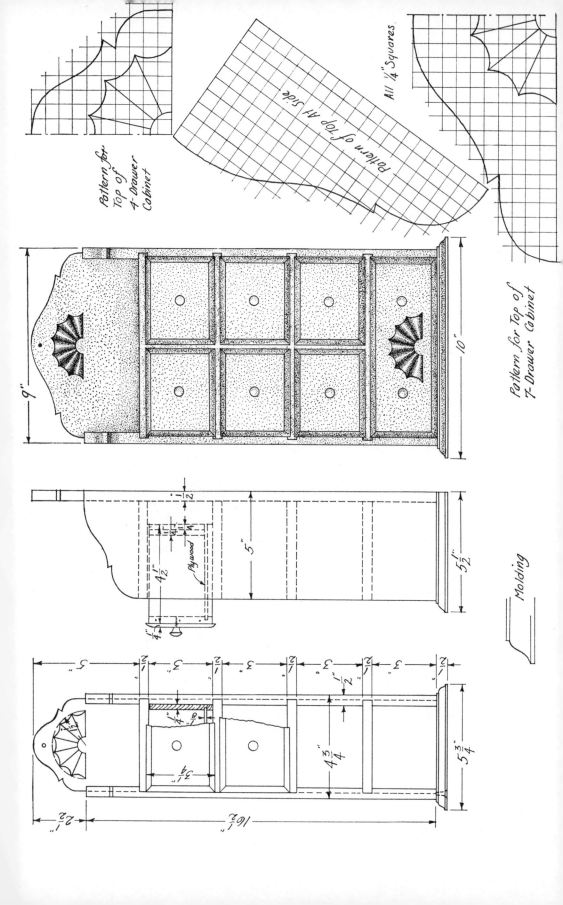

Pattern for Top of 4-Drawer Cabinet

All ¼" Squares

Pattern for Top of A4 Side

Pattern for Top of 7-Drawer Cabinet

9"

10"

Molding

Plywood

½

4½"

4"

¼"

5"

5½"

5"

3"

3"

3"

1½"

2½"

2½"

2½"

2½"

1½"

¼"

⅛"

4¾"

3¼"

4¾"

5¾"

16½"

2½"

Fan-Shaped Box

In the fan-shaped box (Fig. 122), we have a very simple type of ornament which, however, expresses a great deal. An element which enters into the making of the box should be mentioned here. Before carving the fanned out ribs, or even laying out the pattern to carve them, the box top should be shaped as indicated on the front view of Figure 123, where with arrows pointing to them are shown profiles of the flutes, beads, and fillets. This preliminary shaping should be to the upper dotted line.

The front of the box is cut on the band saw from a plank 1 in. thick. The top also is carved from a band-sawed piece ½ in. thick. We believe

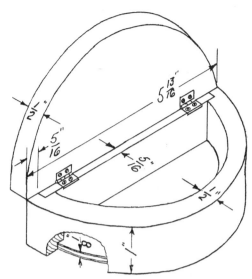

Fig. 121. Construction details.

the construction of the box is made sufficiently clear in Figure 121 to need

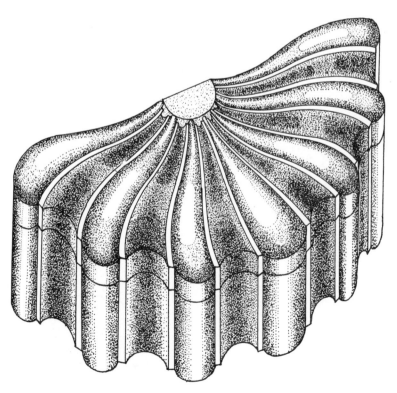

Fig. 122. The fan-shaped box.

little further comment here. If the finish is to be gold paint, or gold leaf, as is often the case in a box of this kind, the box may be carved of softwood like white pine. A box carved of walnut, mahogany, or birch, and finished in a natural color would make a very nice jewelry box, or by doubling the dimensions, a sewing box.

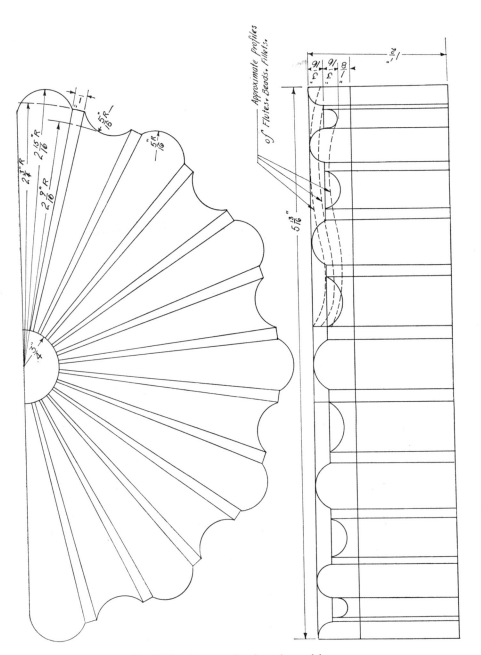

Fig. 123. Pattern for fan-shaped box.

Pipe Holder

Figure 124 shows an interesting pipe holder with the same kind of carving as the fan-shaped box. The base should be turned on the lathe, or shaped by hand separately, and then glued to the carved part. To make it, take a block of hardwood 2½ by 2½ by 4½ in. with the grain running vertically, and saw it first to the shape of the profile shown in the upper view of Figure 124. Next, hollow out the place to hold the pipe, making it to fit the particular pipe you want it to hold. Then carve it, as shown in both views of Figure 124. A natural finish would be most suitable for a pipe holder.

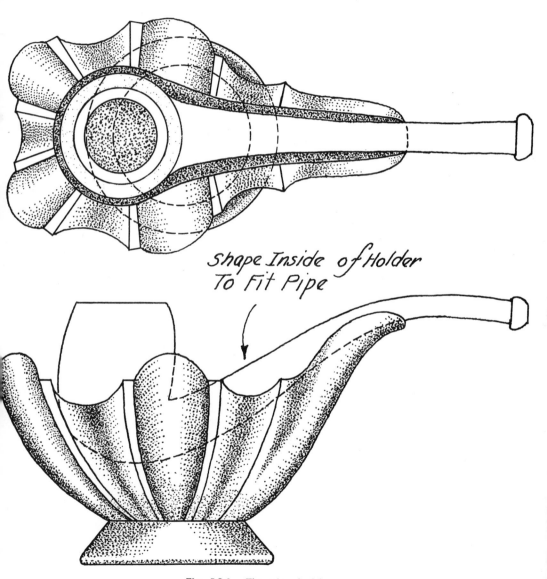

Shape Inside of Holder To Fit Pipe

Fig. 124. The pipe holder.

Bookends
With Acanthus Leaf

Bookends lend themselves readily to being carved, and a nice pair will be very decorative. If one has some nicely bound, favorite volumes, which one wants to display, there is no better way to do it than to put them between a pair of attractively carved bookends.

A stunning pair of bookends are those on which the dew droplets appear on the acanthus leaves. This design (Figs. 125 and 126) is well balanced by the occult method instead of bisymmetrically. This feature, together with the most interesting pattern, occasioned by the variegated serrations on the leaf, the play of light and shade resulting from the considerable amount of modeling on the surface, gives this design considerable distinction.

Make the blocks of wood needed to shape them as shown in Figure 126. Trace the pattern (Fig. 127) and either cut a stencil, or transfer the drawing directly from the tracing to the wood. Mahogany was used to carve the pair shown, but walnut would do equally well.

Outline the design very carefully. Do not cut outlining chisel cuts very deep until some of the background has been removed. Model most of the leaf before starting the beaded water droplets. Make fairly deep V-shaped grooves alongside each rib in the leaf, then round these carefully with the heel of the skew chisel. Follow the modeling on Figure 126 as closely as possible, since it is an improvement on the design in the photograph, which was done a few years ago.

Fig. 125. Book end.

When starting to carve the beads, do not try to separate the beads from each other at first. Instead, cut a deep V-shaped groove clear around the group. Then make short V cuts at angles of 60 degrees from the center to the grooves on either side, making square beads at first. Make them octagon shaped next by trimming the corners carefully, and finally round them as shown. Considerable care must be used to prevent chipping off a bead when this is being done.

Finish up by smoothing all background areas very carefully. The bookends may be finished in natural wood by rubbing on repeated coats of boiled linseed oil, and polishing each one vigorously. Soak the wood thoroughly in oil in a well-heated room. Then rub the wood with several applications of powdered pumice stone to help fill the pores of open-grained woods and give a very smooth finish.

As indicated in Figure 126, the bookends may be weighted by pouring hot lead into holes bored into the bottoms. Green felt may then be glued to the bottoms.

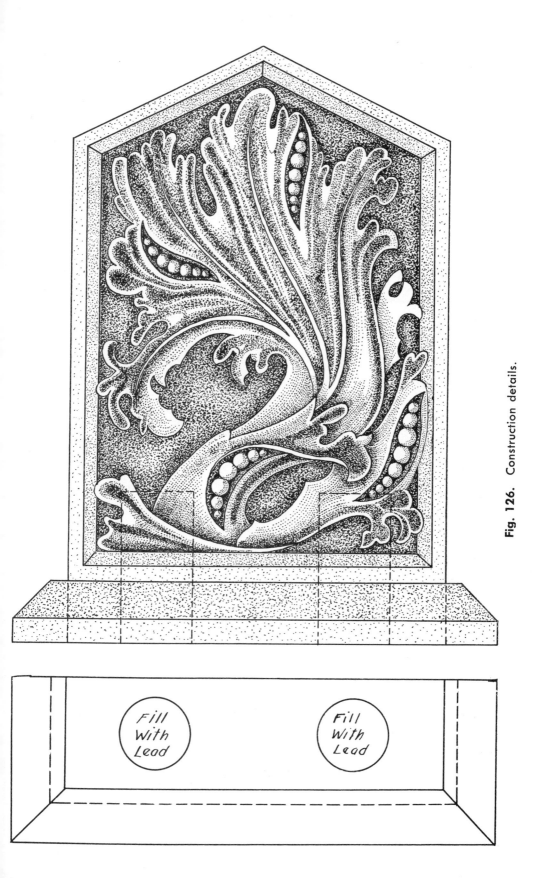

Fig. 126. Construction details.

Fig. 127. Full-size pattern for bookends.

Paper, Letter, and Pencil Holder

The paper, letter, and pencil holder (Fig. 128) is an interesting small project, not too difficult to construct or carve. For this reason it is a good project for a beginner to attempt modeling leaves and scrolls — motifs found in much hand-carved work.

The two lyre-shaped upright pieces holding the envelopes or stationery should be made first. Make the base last, so the grooves may be adjusted to the thickness of the uprights after the carving has been done. The grain of the wood from which the carved pieces are made should run vertically. Walnut is especially good wood to use for this project since it is tough enough not to break easily at the cross-grained, curved, upper bar. These curved bars could be made separately of wood on which the grain runs in a horizontal direction, and could be glued at each end to the other piece. But the author believes it better to make the entire lyre of one piece.

Holes for the dowels should be drilled before the open part in the middle is sawed out. It is also better to do the carving before sawing out the middle part. In that way there will be little or no strain, and consequently, little chance of breaking this weakest part. Once the dowels have been glued into place they will strengthen the crossbar considerably.

Trace the pattern (Fig. 129) and transfer it to the wood. A stencil pattern (see page 32) for this design is shown in Figure 30. Outline the design, including the leaves and scrolls, with chisel cuts, or cut a little outside the lines at first with the V tool, and later trim with the other chisels exactly to the line. The molding of the leaves is made clear in the drawing. Carve the beads in the same manner

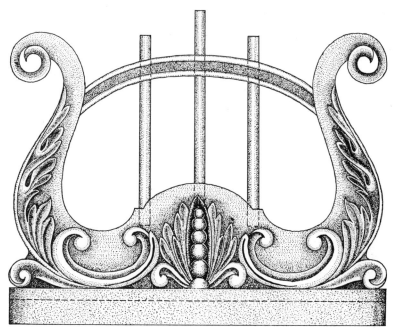

Fig. 128. The paper, letter, and pencil holder.

Pattern

Fig. 129. Full-size pattern for the holder.

110

as was described for carving those on the bookends with the Acanthus Leaf (page 106).

Once the carved members have been completed, make the base, grooving it to hold the carved members which should be glued fast to the grooves. Also cut the pencil grooves, which be-

ing semicircular may be cut with carving chisels.

A natural finish will look well; but the decorative possibilities of carefully rubbed on and blended smudges of color, if the coloring is not overdone, should not be overlooked.

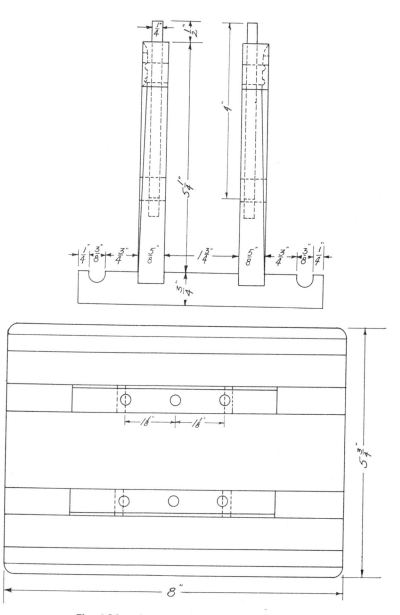

Fig. 130. Construction details of holder.

Carved Box With Beading on Top

The carved box with the beading on top is distinctly French in feeling (Fig. 131). A feature of this box is the lovely shaping on three of its sides. The back is straight in order to permit hinging of the lid. The full-size pattern is shown in Figure 132.

First construct the box as shown. No nails should be used in putting it together, so the sides may be sawed to the contour shown before carving it. This sawing may be done on the band saw. The saw marks may then be removed with carving chisels, or with files and sandpaper.

While at first glance this design may seem complicated and, therefore, difficult to carve, it should really prove quite simple to carve, because the leaves and scrolls may be cut with long sweeps of the tool (Fig. 132). These long cuts cause very little trouble if the proper types of wood are used, and if the tools are kept sharp. Hard maple, walnut, or mahogany would certainly carve well. Softer wood may be used but will be more difficult to carve. Carve the beads according to the instructions given for carving beads on the acanthus leaf bookends (page 106). Be sure in this case to make the beads as round as you possibly can.

Boxes like this are often covered entirely with gold leaf, and are often used as jewelry boxes. Many other uses can be found for a box as attractive as this one. Gold paint may be substituted but it will not hold its color like genuine gold leaf. A natural finish, or tinting with oil paints, or with water colors, offers interesting possibilities.

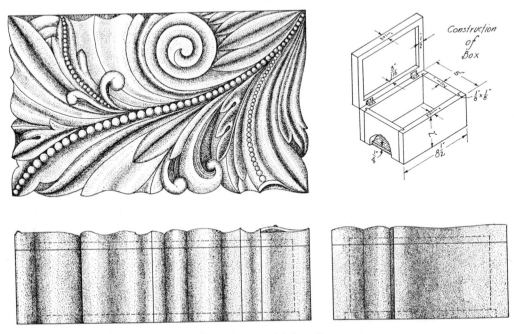

Fig. 131. Carved box with beading on top.

Fig. 132. Full-size pattern for box.

Paper Knife

The paper knife (Fig. 133) is an interesting little project which may be carved with nothing more than a sharp pocketnife. It should be sawed to shape on a jig saw, or with a coping saw before carving is begun. Hardwood like maple, walnut, or hickory should be used.

To carve the handle, first form it to the contour shown in the two views (Fig. 133). Then sketch in all details, such as scales, fins, eyes, and mouth. Outline each of these elements with the point of the knife, then shape them as shown. In carving the scales, cut deepest where the shading is darkest. No part of the design should be cut very deep, but only deep enough to give definite shape to each detail. Do not lose sight of the fact that the handle is to be held in the hand, and that the feel of it should not give discomfort. Therefore, even those parts that stick out, like the fins, should be softened enough so as to feel comfortable in the hand which is holding it.

Fig. 133. The paper knife.

Salad Fork and Salad Spoon

What we have just said of the paper knife also applies to the salad fork (Fig. 134) and the salad spoon (Fig. 135). Once the fork and spoon have been sawed to shape, they may be carved or whittled with a sharp pocketknife. Wood-carving chisels may be used to carve certain parts of the spoon and fork, but a knife may be used to good advantage to do the greater part of the job. Again in the design of the handles, considerable thought has gone into making them fit the hand comfortably.

The leaf, beads, and scroll are carved only after the handles, the bowl of the spoon, and the tines of the fork have been cut to the form of their profile as shown in the top and side views. The V grooves on the front of each handle should be done last. Lines for these should be very carefully laid out, and careful cutting should be done to make them just right.

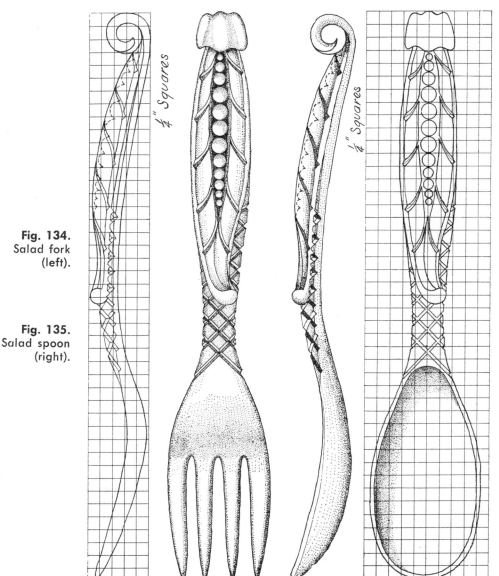

Fig. 134.
Salad fork
(left).

Fig. 135.
Salad spoon
(right).

Carved Boxes

Objects turned on a wood lathe often are well adapted for carving. The small round wooden cannister-like boxes (Figs. 138–140) show the interesting possibilities of using boxes of the same size and shape, but carving them in a variety of ways. These boxes can be used to hold stamps, paper clips, thumbtacks, rubber bands, and other desk accessories.

Figure 141 has a dimensioned drawing for turning a small box to hold a roll of postage stamps. Any wood which is suitable for wood turning may be used, such as maple, birch, walnut, mahogany, or red gum. These woods also carve quite well.

A cylinder long enough to make several of these boxes may be turned on the lathe to a diameter of 2 in. The flanges to which the lids are fitted may also be turned before each box is sawed from the cylinder. After sawing all of the boxes from the cylinder, holes may be bored to hollow the inside. This may be done with an ordinary auger bit if the hole is no larger than 1 in. in diameter, as is the case of the stamp box. A Forstner bit may be used to finish the bottom of the hole to eliminate the hole left by the lead screw of the auger bit.

An easier way to bore the hole is on a drill press with round-shank bits especially made for the purpose. The author has made sets of such bits from regular auger bits by filing off the screw threads on the lead screw and cutting off the square part of the shank so they may be fastened in a Jacob's chuck.

When the large hole has been bored into the stamp box, drill the smaller hole for the dowel which holds the roll of stamps. Before gluing this dowel into the hole, a thin saw kerf (Fig. 141) should be cut, through which the stamps may be pulled from the box.

If a box is made, with the hole no larger than the one in the stamp box, spindle-turning the cylinder is as good a method as any. The facilities for boring a 1-in. hole are usually available in the home workshop. Larger holes, such as those in the other boxes shown here are not so easily drilled or bored into a cylinder as small as these. There is always the problem of how to prevent splitting the cylinder.

Small boxes with holes as large in diameter as these may best be turned by fastening the block of wood to a small faceplate. These usually have provisions for holding the work in the center with a single large wood screw. By turning both the outside and hollowing the inside of the box on a faceplate, you may make sure that the hole will be exactly centered in the middle of the cylinder.

Hollowing out lids like the ones on these boxes, usually involves chuck turning. A number of lids may be cut from a single cylinder of the same diameter as the one from which the boxes were made. Even the doming of the lid on the outside may be done in the cutting off process. The hollowing of the underside of the lid is done by fastening a wooden chuck, as shown in Figure 142, to a faceplate, and then cutting a hole into it with turning tools, just large enough to hold the lid firmly in place with a friction fit.

116

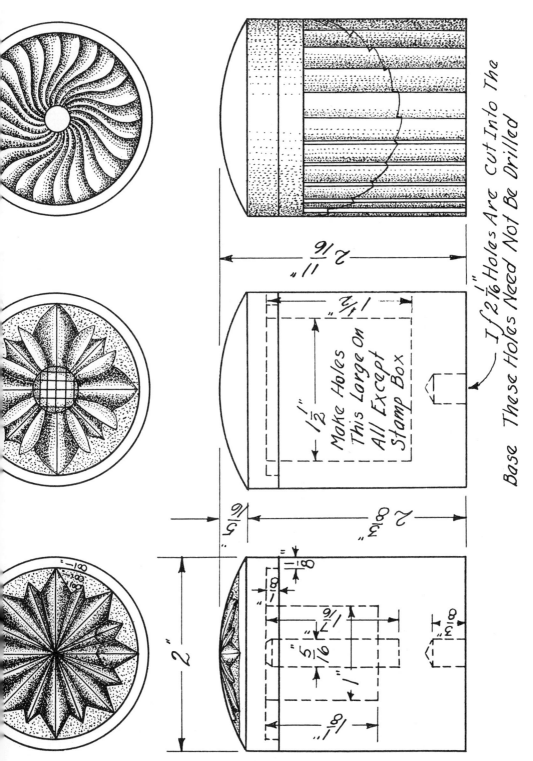

If 2 7/16" Holes Are Cut Into The
Base These Holes Need Not Be Drilled

Make Holes
This Large On
All Except
Stamp Box

2 11/16"

1 1/4"

1 1/2"

2 3/8"

5/16"

2"

1/8"

1/8"

1 1/16"

5/16"

1"

1 1/8"

1 3/8"

Fig. 138.   Construction and design of boxes.

117

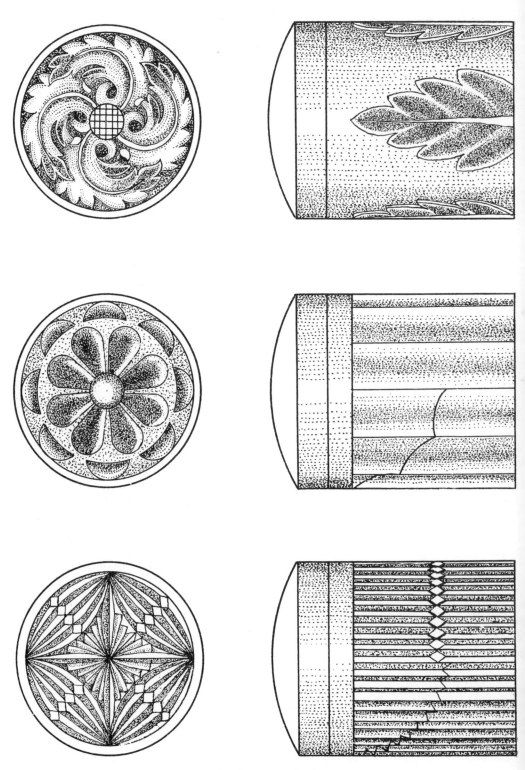

Fig. 139. Designs for boxes.

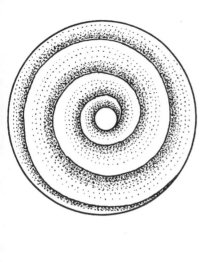

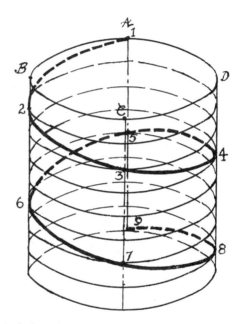

Shows How To Lay Out A Spiral Curve Around A Cylindrical Object.

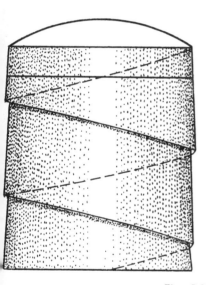

Fig. 140. A spiral design.

In this way the lid may be hollowed out to fit the top of the box perfectly. This method also makes it possible to turn the underside of the lid without damaging the lid in any way. Boxes, cut from a spindle turning, may, of course, be hollowed out on such a chuck in exactly the same manner.

If a set composed of a number of such boxes is made, a stand, or base to hold them might be nice to have.

Holes large enough to set the boxes down into them may be cut into such a base with a hole saw on a drill press, or may be chiseled out with wood-carving tools. An alternate method of holding the boxes (Fig. 138) requires a hole to be drilled into the bottom of the box. This hole fits over a dowel glued to the stand.

Quite a variety of carved designs is shown for the boxes. Many of the

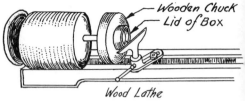

Wooden Chuck
Lid of Box

Wood Lathe

Fig. 142. Using the lathe.

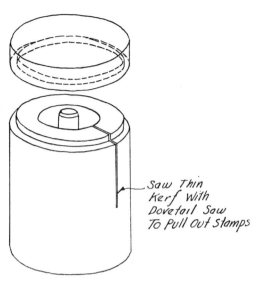

Saw Thin
Kerf With
Dovetail Saw
To Pull Out Stamps

Fig. 141. Box for holding roll
of postage stamps.

motifs are simple and may readily be carved with a sharp knife. The designs shown in Figure 139 (center and right) are more easily done with carving chisels.

The box at left in Figure 139 makes use of chip carving. Chip carving is more easily done with a knife than with chisels. Another interesting design is the spiraled motif (Fig. 140). The method of laying out a spiral such as this for carving is illustrated in

Figure 140. The outside of the cylinder is first divided into four equal parts around its circumference. To do this, cut a piece of paper long enough to reach entirely around the cylinder. Divide this paper with parallel vertical lines into four equal parts. With this paper wrapped around the cylinder, mark A, B, C, D, and through these four points draw vertical lines. The pitch of the spiral will depend upon how far apart you space the lines which you now draw around the circumference of the cylinder. In the example, the lines are spaced ¼ in. apart. The spiral may then be drawn by starting at A which is also the starting point, 1, of the spiral. Going around the cylinder a quarter turn (90 degrees), the spiral drops ¼ in., in going from one circumference circle to the next one below it.

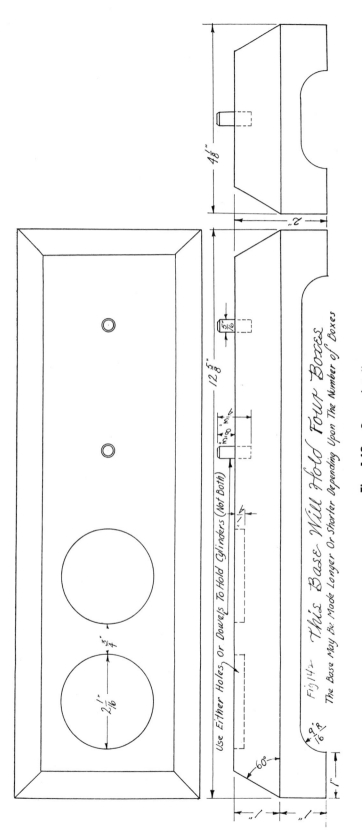

Fig. 143. Base details.

Fruit Bowl

Another design on which spiraled carving is featured is the Baroque fruit bowl in Figure 144. The method of laying out the spiral for the shaft of this bowl is shown in Figure 145. Since we have just finished describing a method for laying out such a spiral on a cylinder, we feel that it will not be necessary to do it again for this project; for while the spiral has a much sharper pitch and is carved differently, the method of laying it out on the shaft is the same as that described on page 120.

The bowl of this project has carving on it similar to that found on the fan-shaped box (Fig. 122). To lay out the fluted and reeded areas, draw two concentric circles, one with a diameter of 9¼ in., which is the diameter of the outside of the bowl, and the other having a diameter of 2 in., which is the diameter of the top of the shaft. The larger circle is divided as shown in Figure 146, and lines are drawn from each point where the flutes, reeds, and fillets meet each other, to the common center of the two circles. You then will have determined the points for drawing the dividing lines of each sector at both its greatest and its smallest width. You will still have to determine the length of each sector, which you cannot get from the drawing with the two concentric circles you have just made. After turning the bowl over, however, a narrow strip of paper reaching from the 2-in. circle drawn at its base, to the top of the bowl on the outside, will give you the correct length. With these data — viz., the length of each

Fig. 144. The fruit bowl.

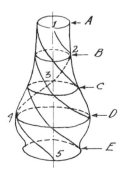

Fig. 145. Laying out the spiral.

flute, or reed; its greatest and its smallest width — you will be able to cut paper patterns and accurately draw the dividing lines.

The bowl and shaft of the fruit bowl were carved of black walnut, while the base was made of hard-rock maple. Mahogany, birch, walnut, or maple are the most suitable woods to carve this very lovely fruit bowl.

122

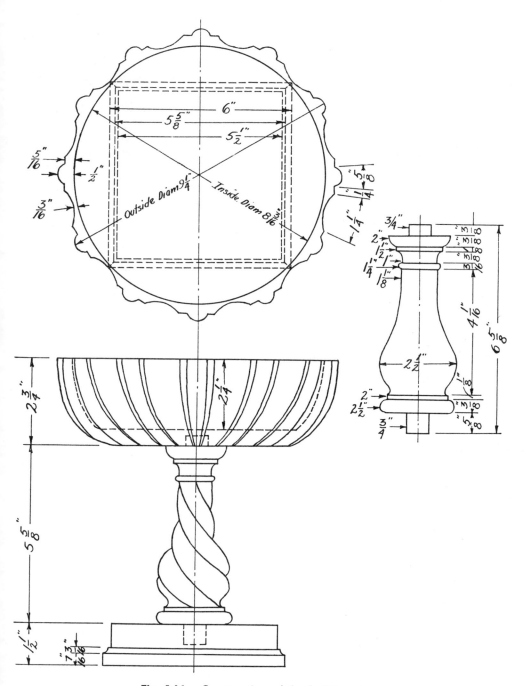

Fig. 146. Construction of the fruit bowl.

Occasional Table

The occasional table (Fig. 147) is a Brothers Adam type in which classical ornament is used for the carving. The egg-and-dart molding, a favorite with designers who work in the classical tradition, was used around the edge of the octagon-shaped table top. Our interpretation of this molding is not difficult to carve, but the spacing of each unit must be carefully laid out.

The drawing (Fig. 149) shows how the apron, legs, and small blocks which alternate with the legs at the ends of the stretchers are joined together. Tenons are perpendicular to the angled ends of each stretcher instead of running parallel with the grain. A dimensioned detail of the blocks, legs, stretchers, and joints is shown in the drawing. This makes it easy to cut the mortises on a mortising machine, or by hand, and the angled tenon is just as easy to cut by hand as a straight one would be. The important thing when making these joints is to make a good tight fit. Then, when the joints are glued up, ordinary bar clamps may be used to pull them tightly together.

The table frame consists of four legs, four blocks, and eight stretchers. When all joints are made, you first glue one block and one leg to the ends of four of the stretchers, doing it as shown in the drawing (Fig. 148). When the glue has thoroughly hardened, the last four stretchers may be glued to these assembled parts. The eighth stretcher will have to be fitted from above to mortises cut to the top of the leg and block. Clamps need be used on the outside of the frame only to do this last step in the gluing process, but small triangular-

Fig. 147. The occasional table.

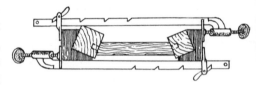

Fig. 148. Gluing the frame.

shaped strips of wood should be placed between the clamps and the wood when pulling the joints together, to prevent damaging the legs or blocks.

While the table top may be without the glass, this one had the middle recessed deep enough to hold a piece of double-strength glass, under which was placed a beautifully designed, hand-dyed piece of silk. A similar design could be painted on paper, and would serve the same purpose. The full-size designs for the carving are shown in Figures 150–152.

This table may be used as a bedside table, or for a number of other purposes. The wood used to make it was mahogany.

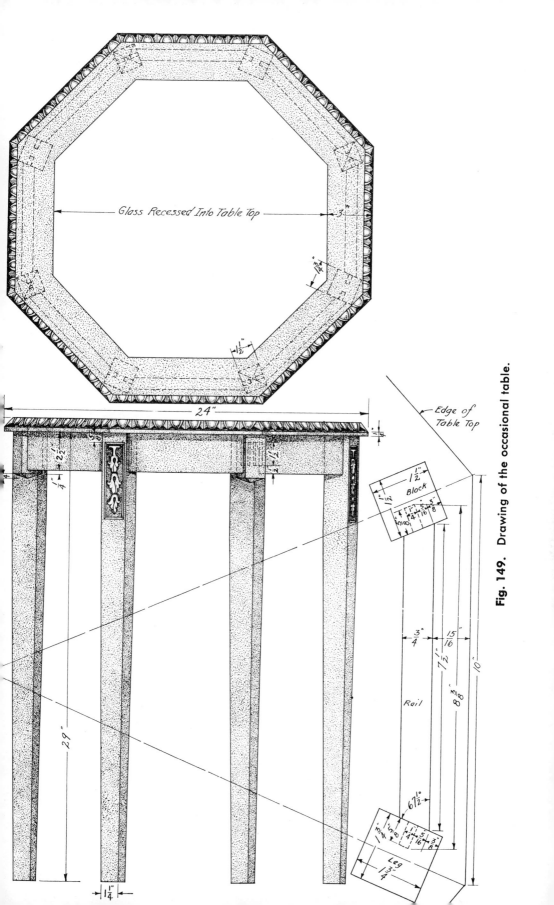

Glass Recessed Into Table Top

3"

3"/4

1 1/2"

3"

24"

Glass Recessed Into Table Top

Edge of
Table Top

1 1/2"
Block

Rail

Leg

Fig. 149. Drawing of the occasional table.

Fig. 150. Full-size pattern for leg design.

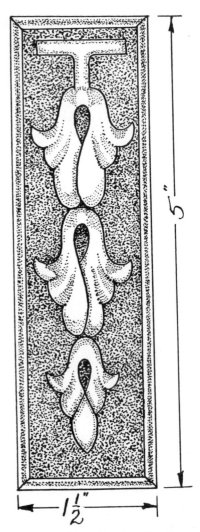

Fig. 151. Carving detail for leg design.

Fig. 152. Egg and dart molding detail.

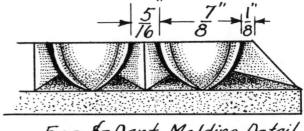

Egg-&-Dart Molding Detail

Venetian Mirror

A really lovely thing to carve is the Venetian mirror frame (Fig. 153). It may be made larger than shown, if so desired, or smaller for that matter, simply by enlarging or reducing the graph squares in Figure 154, thus enlarging or reducing the pattern.

One of the difficulties encountered in making a mirror of this kind is shaping the glass to an irregularly curved outline. The dotted lines in Figure 154 simplify the shape about as much as possible, and if a plain glass mirror is used, this outline may be reproduced as shown. A curve must be ground into even such a simplified outline (see arrow) on a grinding wheel. Shops equipped to replace glass on automobiles usually grind glass, but it

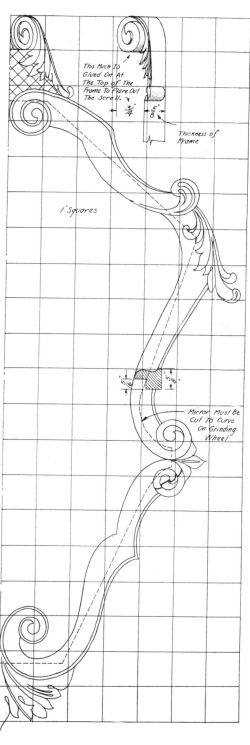

Fig. 153. The Venetian mirror.

Fig. 154. Construction details.

is ordinarily best to send a paper pattern to a shop which specializes in making mirrors to fit any kind of frame.

If the mirror is to have the glass beveled, and a beveled plate glass mirror will certainly enhance its beauty, then the outline of the pattern must duplicate the outline of the inside of the frame, with about ¼ in. added all around.

The frame of the mirror should be cut from one piece. Mahogany, walnut, or some other strong and tough hardwood is recommended, but sometimes a softer wood, such as white pine is used, and when carved it is covered entirely with gold leaf. Patterns for doing the carving are given in Figure 155.

Fig. 155. Patterns for the mirror carving.

37   762IDA BR 3289
10/94 30910-30